I NEED TO F⬛⬛ING TALK TO YOU!

To Bart

Fxxxing Enjoy!

Russ

THE ART OF NAVIGATING DIFFICULT WORKPLACE CONVERSATIONS

BY KEN CAMERON AND RUSSELL STRATTON

| CORPORATE CULTURE SHIFT    Bluegem
Learning

"Sometimes conversations suck, but you need to have them, and this book lays out how. Russell and Ken have put together and road-tested simple, up-front, and thoughtful approaches to awkward and difficult workplace conversations."

— **Andrew Phung**, actor, *Kim's Convenience*

TABLE OF CONTENTS

ISBN: 978-1-7773026-0-3

PROLOGUE

Let's get one thing straight off the top

"I need to f**xxx**ing talk to you", is a bad way to start any conversation, let alone one with a co-worker. Unfortunately, too many of us have started conversations this way, even if we haven't quite gone so far as to drop an F-bomb in the middle of the office.

So why is this commonly happening in the workplace? Usually it's because some issue has been festering for weeks or months and it has finally reached the point where we can't stand it anymore. One last straw has broken the proverbial camel's back and we've just f**xxx**ing lost it! Often the employee has been told about the problem over and f**xxx**ing over again, yet still nothing has changed. Our internal dialogue becomes a stream of frustrated thoughts; *do they re-*

ally think they can get away with acting like this and making my life miserable? If they think I'm not serious about the consequences, then that fxxxing fxxx has another fxxxing thing coming. This shouldn't come as a surprise, because I have been perfectly fxxxing clear with them!

But have we really?

Too many managers approach a conversation in which they must challenge difficult behaviour with a lot of trepidation. We often begin our workshops by asking participants why this is the case and we hear the same answers repeatedly. Our participants tell us they are afraid of angry reactions on the part of the employee. Alternatively, they know what they want to say, but once the employee is in front of them, they get tongue-tied. Perhaps they know what they want to say, but instead they package it up in the dreaded feedback sandwich; layering constructive feedback between two examples of positive feedback. This convolutes the importance of the area that requires improvement.

The result is we aren't direct. We beat around the bush and try to soften the blow to avoid an adverse reaction. Maybe we didn't see the actual behaviour in question, so we are relying on hearsay, or we've become lost in an argument over the details of what really happened. Often, we know we need to continue to work with the person or we want them to like us, so we try to keep it light.

Sometimes out of necessity to keep a project progressing it's inevitable that we offer to help; only to find ourselves now taking responsibility to complete their work by the time they've left our office. Even though it's not very clear what they're going to do about changing their behaviour, we validate ourselves with the thought *hey, at least we brought it up with them. If they continue to be this unmanageable, then next time, we'll really lay down the law.* So when the next time comes around and the individual exhibits the same behaviour, we feel it's completely reasonable that we just f**xxx**ing lose it!

If this has been your approach in the past, you're not doing anyone any favours.

Are People Really Fxxxing Unmanageable?

Before we proceed any further let's dispel a myth now; there is no such thing as an employee who is truly unmanageable. Thinking of these individuals as "f**xxx**ing unmanageable", is unfairly demonizing them, and unfairly positioning yourself as a victim or martyr. It may feel good, but it rarely positions you as a strong and reliable leader[1].

Russell begins almost every one of our Forum Theatre for Business workshops by saying "I'll let you in on a secret. In my twenty-five years of managing teams and developing other managers, I have realized that most people want to do a good job."

We usually have at least one participant who responds with "You need to come to *my* workplace."

You might be having the same thoughts. *There are some people who are inherently lazy, who are naturally disaffected, who are just so f**xxx**ing antagonistic that they're impossible*

[1] It's unlikely (though not impossible) that you have an employee who is behaving like this for the sole purpose of making your life miserable. If that is the case, then what you may have is an employee exhibiting sociopathic behaviours. If you suspect that this is what you're dealing with then we'll refer you to *The Sociopath Next Door*, by clinical psychologist and former Harvard faculty member Martha Stout, PhD. Don't take this as an easy out, it's a last resort.

to work with and I've been stuck with one of them. This person is beyond hope.

If that is the case, put this book down and go ahead and fire them. It will be easier and less painful in the long run.

Before you say, *HR would never allow it or the union would make my life miserable or they're the boss's favourite,* consider the possibility that you're lying to yourself. If their behaviour truly is unmanageable, you can figure it out.

Ask yourself, was this problematic employee lazy, or disaffected or antagonistic when they started at the organization? Most employees develop their behaviour over time, as a response to some dissatisfaction or disillusionment with their work. They may have been mistreated in the past and are now distrustful. They may have good ideas, but they've been worn down because no one listens or they view the structures and systems as needlessly cumbersome. All of this can usually be boiled down to a reaction against change.

Resistance to change is another precursor to difficult behaviour. When we say "change" we mean any sort of deviation from the way things were. This could be extreme like a complete re-organization or it could be as simple as introducing a new computer program for tracking inventory. Other examples could be a change in the individual's workstation, or the addition of a new team member.

People respond to change in different ways. Some embrace change with an enthusiastic "YES" and feel energized, challenged and renewed. Others respond with an outright "NO" and feel drained, challenged and dispirited. Between these two poles, there is an infinite spectrum of response.

Once you uncover and understand the change they are reacting against, you may find you can empathize with them. Empathizing with your employee makes the conversation easier. It makes them better listeners and it makes YOU a better coach.

Recently Ken mentored briefly under Peter Hinton, a brilliant theatre director who served for many years as Artistic Director of The National Arts Centre of Canada. Peter claimed that he doesn't believe in "talent". There is a prevailing belief in society that talent is some inherent mysterious force; you either have it or you don't. The Ancient Greek and Roman societies even believed talent was a gift from the gods. But this idea is dangerously false and even destructive. "If we assume that some actors have talent and others don't," Peter explains, "then there's nothing a director can do for them. I might as well give up."

Instead, Peter is one of those who chooses to believe that everyone has talent. "Some actors simply have something that blocks them, some internal obstacle that gets in their way. This allows me to assist them by investigating what those obstacles might be. When we uncover it together, I can aid them in removing those blocks so their talent can flow freely."

By the same reasoning, if you suppose that some employees "just fit in", while others simply "aren't team players", then there is nothing you can do to coach them. You might as well give up now and begin the process of firing them. And what kind of leader does that make you?

If, on the other hand, you begin to think of your employee as temporarily experiencing a behaviour that is getting in the way of their ability to do a good job, then possibilities for great performance emerge.

Here's what you need to do. Separate the behaviour from the individual. And here's why you need to do it.

- **It builds empathy**. Reframe your unmanageable employee as a colleague who needs support. Then you can reframe yourself as someone who can help.

- **It's constructive**. Behaviours are tangible. Now you can generate a list of actual problems to address.

- **It's engaging**. Build an action plan that sets them up for success. Their self-interest will get them engaged.

- **It's participatory**. When you view them as someone with the potential to transform, you enrol them as partners in change.

Once you separate the individual from the behaviour, you can begin to view your employees as well-intentioned colleagues who are trapped in a cycle that needs to be addressed.

THE FOUR HATS

If we agree that it's not effective to think of our employees as "fxxxing unmanageable, flawed individuals" for whom there is little hope, then we need a new language; one free of F-bombs and other gratuitous swear words. We find it useful to think of your employee as wearing a hat that epitomizes the behaviour they're exhibiting.

Behaviours are constant but hats are not. You can remove a hat and exchange it for another. With the proper encouragement, your employee can trade in their poor behaviour for another behaviour that's more productive. Just like a hat, behaviours can become overly comfortable if they are worn too long. And like a hat, a behaviour can get shabby if not exchanged regularly.

We've chosen four hats to illustrate four categories of behaviour. Let's go through these four hats one at a time.

THE VIKING HELMET

No = (No Negative)
This person is willing to listen but is ready to react negatively at the drop of a hat.

I Am Resistant
I am defending a certain pattern or status quo. I have an aggressive or passive aggressive approach to change.

The individual wearing a Viking helmet, is usually defending a certain pattern or status quo that is precious to them in some way. Like a Viking who suddenly finds themselves transported into the modern world, this individual is clinging to old gods.

In other words, they are attached to an old way of life that is outdated; new approaches confuse them and cause them to lash out. This may take the form of aggressive behaviour, or it could also be a passive aggressive response.

For example:
- "I've tried it and it doesn't work."
- "This isn't my fault."
- "It's not in my job description."

Their response is not just no, it's **no negative** for extra emphasis.

THE SUN HAT

No + (No Positive)
This person is so disengaged they might as well be reading a trashy novel on the beach.

I Am Contented
My present situation feels good enough as it is. I have no reason to change.

This person's response is not quite as negative as The Viking Helmet, so we call this a **no positive**. Of course, such a person rarely says "no" outright, so you have to listen for the "no" buried within their comments.

For example:

- "I am on target, so what's the fuss?"
- "If it ain't broke, don't fix it."
- "I've always been good at this."

You can see how this individual is rationalizing their "no". In fact, it's important to realize that they most likely believe what they're saying. They really do believe they are on target and it isn't broken! In short, they feel their present situation is good enough as is. This person has no realization that there's a need for change.

THE HARD HAT

Yes – (Yes Negative)
This person is ready to work hard but needs clear direction to overcome inertia.

I Am Willing
I'm willing to change but I don't know how. Help me figure out what to do to move forward.

Let's say you've persuaded one of your team members to remove their Sun Hat or set aside their Viking Helmet. Now they've adopted another piece of headgear, a construction worker's yellow Hard Hat. We label this person as a **yes negative**.

For example:

- "How can I achieve my targets?"
- "I've got an idea, but I need permission to try."
- "What if we did it this way?"

The hard-hatted individual is willing to change but does not know how or what to do to move forward. This can be a bit frustrating at times because they require monitoring. They need your support because, left to their own devices, they may revert to Viking or Sun Hat behaviour. But this is a good employee to have because they can be coached. There is an opportunity here to be creative with them and to brainstorm a solution together.

THE GRADUATE CAP

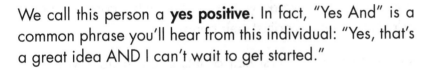

Yes + (Yes Positive)
This individual is really starting to deliver high performance.

I Am Innovative
I'm all over this. I'll have it on your desk by morning.

We call this person a **yes positive**. In fact, "Yes And" is a common phrase you'll hear from this individual: "Yes, that's a great idea AND I can't wait to get started."

For example:

- "I'm going to do this. And I'll do it on this schedule. I'll report back when it's done."

- "100% we can make this happen, the issue is how can we achieve even MORE?"

- "Nothing can hold me back!"

This is the employee we all want to have! Not unlike a wind-up toy, you can wind them up, let them go and focus on your own work. However, be careful and don't get too confident in their abilities. As we'll see, they still require some management.

Out of necessity our categories are broad. We acknowledge that these four hats are likely to come in an infinite number of colours, shapes and sizes. After all, there's no one size fits all when it comes to hats, just as with people. However, categorization is useful. Metaphors provide us with a lens by which to refocus our perceptions of the world. These tools are meant to give you a place to start a discussion.

I Can't Work With You When You're Like This

When dealing with the Sun Hat and the Viking Helmet, the first two hats on our spectrum, many leaders will dedicate their energies to coaching these individuals by offering empathy or logic.

This is a fool's errand.

A Sun Hat and a Viking Helmet can't simply be coached on how to work effectively with change. From the perspective of the Sun Hat and Viking Helmet, change isn't necessary and may even be counterproductive. A standard coaching approach won't work with someone who can't or won't admit they need to adjust their behaviour.

As we'll see in the first half of this book, initially you must make Sun Hats and Viking Helmets aware of their behaviour and its effect on others. Only once they accept these facts and embrace the need for change, will they be in a position for your coaching to have a positive impact.

These are the things we're not saying in difficult workplace conversations. There are ways we can say it better, and with greater clarity, so that the message sinks in and your employees are more likely to remove their hats and get to work.

The decision to have a conversation is the first and most important decision you need to make. Already after reading the prologue, you've learned you need to successfully separate the behaviour from the person. You've identified what style of hat they're wearing and by extension, what kind of behaviour the person is exhibiting. You've determined the kind of conversation you need to have.

Now you need to decide if you're going to live with this behaviour or if you're going to fix it. There may be good reasons to live with it. The individual may be going through a difficult time for personal reasons, such as a divorce or the declining health of a loved one. The individual may be adjusting to a reorganization or a new way of working. An exciting project may have been shelved or defunded or put on hiatus. All of these may be good reasons to cut your employee some slack.

If you're going to live with this behaviour, then commit to that decision. Be intentional about it and stop complaining about this individual to your colleagues, friends and family. By doing so, you're transferring your own inability or unwillingness to address the issue onto them and once again unfairly demonizing them and positioning yourself as a martyr.

Keep in mind that each of the circumstances we've outlined is, or should be, temporary. It's perfectly ok for any one of us to put on a Viking Helmet or a Sun Hat for a short period of time. We all have bad days so the key words here are "days" and "temporary". You'll want to keep an eye on this individual and their behaviour, and if it doesn't clear up in short order and it isn't resolving itself, then you may need to address it.

The fact is not addressing the behaviour isn't really doing anyone any favours. Sometimes we can fool ourselves into thinking that the problem will go away on its own accord, or that their fellow employees will apply peer pressure to change them, or that they'll figure it out on their own because it's so f**xxx**ing obvious that they're behaving inappropriately. This approach never works. Instead, the opposite happens; usually questionable behaviour starts out as a small irritant but when left unchecked, becomes a major issue that leads to discipline or dismissal. How then, have we supported the employee by not addressing the matter early on? Instead, they would be quite justified in saying they had been blindsided because no one ever told them they were doing anything wrong.

Transferring the person to another department isn't resolving the situation either. In this instance, you're just taking your basket of snakes and handing it to another leader and suggesting that they deal with it. Except for the fact that you're not even giving them the courtesy of *telling* them that you're handing them a basket of snakes. Which means, you're guaranteeing that they'll get bitten as soon as they open the lid. A manager who decides that it isn't their role to address a problem behaviour, is just letting the responsibility slide off their shoulders as if their suit were made of Teflon.

Which means you have a choice to make. You can fix it but the only way to fix behaviour is to challenge it.

SPEAK UP

"You should fire him," said a gruff voice at the back of the room.

"Really?" Ken asked. "Why don't you come up here and show us how it's done."

We were delivering one of our workshops to a room of 30 engineers. They represented a cross-section of middle management business leaders in the twenty-first century that were educated, urban, open-minded, worldly, focused and experienced. They were comfortable identifying their strengths and had initiative to improve their weaknesses.

We hired a popular improv actor named Andrew Phung to play the employee. Andrew is a recognizable actor playing the character "Kimchee" on the popular television series *Kim's Convenience*. He has won two Canadian Screen Actor's awards and is famous across the country. However, on this occasion, Andrew was playing a geologist and each of the engineers was taking a turn as his manager. As each participant came forward and tried to calm him down, Andrew's character was becoming inflexible.

"Seriously," the gruff voice of an experienced engineer we'll call Witek piped up again, "if my employee was that insubordinate, I'd fire them." Witek explained that hierarchy is important in an engineering workplace. "One has to make everyone motivated, yes, sure, but sometimes the law has to be laid down." It was hard to argue against his logic, so Ken asked him to try it out in real time.

Our workshops use a technique called Forum Theatre that has been around since the 1950s. Forum Theatre, sometimes called Theatre of the Oppressed, is the brainchild of pioneering Brazilian theatre director, writer and politician Augusto Boal.

Boal trained as a chemical engineer before chasing his dream of working in the theatre. After graduation, he wrote and directed politically infused agitprop plays and toured around rural Brazil. In these villages, Boal observed a new generation of educators who rejected traditional teaching methods. Instead, this new breed taught their adult pupils how to read and write by focusing on everyday words they could use when they travelled to market. The stickiness of making work that was active and relevant, fascinated Augusto Boal. Over time he realized that his plays were nowhere near as effective at creating significant social and political change.

One day, while presenting a play at a community centre, Augusto Boal snapped. He'd been to this particular location many times with the same play. Every time he came back, the housing situation was worse and the residents more and more disenfranchised. Boal stood up and stopped the actress playing the mother mid-sentence. He asked for input from the audience. He demanded to know how the character should react to the oppressive situation. He pointed at the mother. "What should she do?" Silence. Crickets.

Finally, a disgusted voice shouted from the back of the auditorium. "Speak up!"

It was the cleaning lady. She had seen this same play perhaps a dozen times over the past two or three years. Like Boal, she could put up with the play no longer. She threw down her broom and stormed out.

Boal chased after her. "Wait!" he shouted. "What do you mean?"

"The wife should speak up," the cleaning lady repeated. "So, she can be heard and others know exactly what is needed."

"Show us," Boal urged.

The cleaning lady came onstage and took over the role of the wife. She tore a strip off the landlord and rallied the other characters. When the cleaning lady ran out of ideas, she demanded the audience give her some help and when she was done, Boal encouraged someone else to pick up where she left off. Other audience members leapt onto the stage one after another, emboldened by this cleaning lady who first decided the character should speak up.

The spectator had become the "spect-actor", and Forum Theatre was born.

Fast-forward fifty years to our training centre, when Ken asked Witek to "show us how it's done." Witek groaned at being asked to participate, but he rose and strode to the front of the room. He sat down opposite Andrew and stared him straight in the eye. That's when everything changed.

WITEK: Andrew. I need to fxxxing talk to you. Do you have a family?

ANDREW: Uh. Yes.

WITEK: Children?

ANDREW: A little boy.

WITEK: That's more important than all this. At the end of the day, we all just want to go home to our families. So, Andrew, it's a simple job I'm asking you to do.

ANDREW: I know! It's so simple a monkey could do it! Is that what you think? That I'm a monkey?

WITEK: No. Everyone here respects you.

ANDREW: That's how you show respect in this place? By putting me in a closet at the end of the hall?

WITEK: It's not a closet.

ANDREW: It was a broom closet before it got converted into an office! That's why it has no windows.

WITEK: At the end of the day, we all want to go home to our family.

ANDREW: And when I get home, do you know what I tell them? I say, "Hey, your Daddy is just like Harry Potter. He

spends his day locked in a closet."
And meanwhile, Beverley gets to
finish organizing the seismic shoot
on MY project with MY team. And now
you're telling me I can't go back to
my old team?

WITEK: Maybe I can help with some of your
workload?

Ken called a time out. Witek acknowledged he made a fundamental mistake. He formed a logical argument while standing on the sidelines, however once in the hot seat and faced with Andrew's strong emotion and counterargument, he couldn't nimbly change tactics. By the end of the dialogue, he was volunteering to do Andrew's work for him.

The military have a saying: "No plan survives first contact with the enemy[2]."

Witek's plan didn't consider that strong emotions aren't defused with logic. Someone in Andrew's position is in the heat of the moment, triggered by a deeply held emotional need. This state keeps them from seeing another side of the issue, no matter how rational. To simulate a real-life situation, we instructed Andrew to remain angry until the participant defused it with empathy. His anger was to resurface regularly until the participants unearthed the underlying issue. For the purposes of moving the scene forward and giving Witek an easy win, Andrew handed him a giant

[2] According to Ralph Keyes author of *The Quote Verifier: Who Said What, Where, and When*, this quote has had various attributions through the past three centuries. American leaders adopted it in the early stages of the Iraq war, which led many to falsely attribute it to Dwight D. Eisenhower or George Patton. Others claimed Napoleon said it. Keyes tells us the observation originated with Helmuth Von Moltke in the mid-nineteenth century.

clue at the end of the scene. Did you spot it? Look at the last paragraph. Andrew complains of isolation. He's working in a small windowless office while the rest of the team get to do something much more exciting.

Witek completely missed the clue, because he had already decided on his logical argument. He hadn't been trained to listen and respond.

The Art of Difficult Conversations

Recently we were asked to deliver a workshop on respect in the workplace for a group of 60 front line workers in an oilfield services company. As the workshop began, we noticed the group trudging in and eyeing us warily. Our contact at the company explained that a few years before, the same group sat through a respect in the workplace seminar that consisted of the facilitator reading the entire policy out loud and then asking everyone to sign a form stating they understood it.

This is an extreme example of the kind of f**xxx**ing b**xxx**s**xxx** training that managers regularly suffer through in the business world.

We believe that no leader should have to suffer like this, and we have dedicated our respective companies to making workplace learning engaging and relevant.

Our work together began bleary-eyed, at an early-morning networking event. The two of us share an interest in active, experiential learning. Russell's early experience as a Personnel and Operational Manager in the UK sparked a curiosity that led him to earn a Master's Degree in Human Resource Management, from the University of Northampton. In London, Russell worked with a wide range of organizational cultures. He provided training to all levels, from frontline staff to executive management boards. Among these clients were Her Majesty's Customs and Excise (a.k.a. the UK Customs Service) and Scotland Yard. Both employ simulation as a method to achieve lasting, measurable change in business performance.

Over coffee at that morning networking event, Russell asked Ken if he had ever worked with Forum Theatre. Russell had explored the technique in the UK to train his clients on how to handle difficult situations. That early experience had planted a notion that Forum Theatre could be a powerful way to create good leaders and not bad bosses.

Ken is one of Alberta's leading playwrights, who has penned hit plays performed across Canada. His published works are available around the world. As well, for twenty years he worked as an independent director, producer and arts administrator. At the pinnacle of this phase of his career, Ken was Artistic Director of Canada's national theatre festival. Ken had his first experience with Forum Theatre when he organized a conference in conjunction with his festival and commissioned a theatre director to explore contract negotiation using Forum Theatre techniques.

After leaving the festival, Ken applied these techniques to the corporate boardroom as a group facilitator. When he met Russell, Ken had just completed a stint as "Citizen

Raconteur" for the City of Calgary's Cultural Transformation Project. In that role he helped the city's administration redefine a corporate narrative for its 15,000 employees. Ken was also Artist-in-Corporate-Residence for a leading credit union called First Calgary Financial. There he led 28 senior leaders on a customized 8-week Innovation and Creativity in Business training program. So, like Russell, Ken was deeply engaged with experiential learning.

We began with a simple principle: the best way to learn is by getting participants out of their seats and onto "the stage." In *Make It Stick: The Science of Successful Learning*, Peter Brown points out that many common learning habits, such as listening to a lecture, re-reading, underlining and highlighting create the illusion of mastery, but what is learned fades quickly. More complex and durable learning comes from challenging participants to put their new knowledge into practice and pushing them slightly out of their comfort zone.

When we add an actor skilled in improvisation and trained in Forum Theatre techniques into the mix, then everyone gets pushed out of their comfort zone, including us. Participants get engaged, instructors get nervous and lessons get cemented. We realized that with Forum Theatre, we could get participants as close to real life as possible, without actually having their employees in the room with them. With Forum Theatre, business leaders can make mistakes. The worst thing that can happen is that they'll get their egos slightly bruised, but within this experience, they'll have an opportunity that doesn't exist in the real world; the opportunity to rewind and try again.

From this realization, Forum Theatre for Business was born.

In our workshops we can interview our clients in advance about the issues their managers face in the workplace. These interviews allow us to customize scenarios that are specific to the workplace and resonate with participants. We have found over the years, that it is beneficial to create a scenario that is set in a parallel universe. For each workshop, we create a fictional company that is very close to, but not identical to, our client's company. One client's oil and gas company becomes "Riverside Exploration". Another client's construction company becomes "Riverside Construction". Otherwise we find participants get bogged down in details. They fixate on which processes are different. They spend time explaining to us which regulations prevent or enable certain actions. They tell us which forms need to be filled out, in which order and in what colour pen.

This is not what's important in our workshops.

At the outset of our workshops, Russell usually offers participants a set of tools to effectively prepare for a conversation. He begins with a simple but effective structure, that is memorable even under pressure. Then Ken offers an opportunity to put these skills into practice with our trained actor-improvisers. Participants come to the front of the room one at a time to have a conversation with our live actor. We find that in traditional role-play, peers are matched up with one another and half-heartedly pretend to be another person. No one wants to embarrass themselves, or their partner so participants tend to make it easy on one another, rather than useful for one another.

Our actor-improvisers don't do anything half-hearted, and they don't make it easy. Their training allows them to acquiesce only if they are persuaded to give up their unmanageable behaviour. Participants often work through one problem, only to come up against another. At these moments, Ken can pause the action, call upon other audience members, rewind, and then resume. He invites someone who may have a different tactic in mind to replace the person who is stuck. Our workshops provide participants with an experience as close to real life as possible, though unlike real life, we can pause our scenarios and offer a do-over.

Written Tools for Surviving First Contact

In this book we offer a detailed explanation of the conversation techniques we recommend. Since we can't get you onstage in front of your fellow readers, to simulate the powerful impact of engaging in dialogue, we have adapted four of the most popular scenarios that we use in our workshops. You'll get to watch these conversations unfold and see how the characters struggle to have the conversation that they know they need to have.

In the following pages. you'll meet a cast of 8 characters in 4 different workplaces.

In Act One we'll focus on the Viking Helmet and meet Raj, a Manager at Riverside Exploration who is struggling with Veronique, one of his Geologists. We'll share with you a framework that Raj will use to challenge Veronique's behaviour and convince her to remove her Viking Helmet.

In Act Two, we'll focus on the Sun Hat and meet Kendra, the Director of Culture at the City of Riverside who is working with Alon, the Manager of the Public Art Program. We'll see how Kendra uses the same framework but adapts the challenging conversation to her specific situation.

During the Intermission, we'll introduce you to a coaching model, inventively titled the C.O.A.C.H. Model.

In Act Three, we meet Dean, a Manager at Riverside Construction, who uses the C.O.A.C.H. Model with Mario. Mario is successfully wearing his Hard Hat, but he needs coaching on how he can deal with someone under his direct supervision who is wearing a Sun Hat. In Act Four, we will explore how the C.O.A.C.H. model can be useful in structuring a conversation with Graduate Cap wearing individuals. We'll encounter Andrea, the CEO of Riverside Hospital, who's in a conflict with Luis, the Executive Director of the stand-alone Riverside Hospital Foundation.

In each Act, you'll encounter an exercise, worksheet or other opportunity to help you to envision how the manager could succeed. We will give you some tools to apply to the situation. You'll be able to reimagine how this dialogue should progress. Then we'll offer you a "take two", in which our fictional manager gets a chance to try again. When the text resumes, you'll be able to see if your ideas match up with ours. Yours may be as good as our suggestions, they may be better, or we may share ideas that overlap. That doesn't make your ideas right or wrong; you'll still have gained knowledge from the exercise. Just like the participants in our real-life workshops, you'll be free to make the intellectual leap between these fictional Riverside companies and your own workplace.

Together these techniques and strategies promote analysis, synthesis, and evaluation of the content in ways that allow it to stick with you long after you set the book down.

This means that you can read this book in several ways. You can read it straight through as one would read a novel. This allows you to follow the arc of the leaders as they learn how to manage their employees. You can identify with the employees as they grow under the guidance of their increasingly insightful mentors. Or you can read it as a practical toolkit, in which you choose to stop and methodically complete the exercises. Some exercises may take a few minutes, while others take only a moment. You may want to fill out a worksheet or you may choose to reflect on the exercise mentally for a few moments.

However, there's one thing we strongly recommend; don't be shy to write in this book. It's not going to become a collector's item. We know. We wrote it. Something different happens to our brains when we write things down or mark up a text. The act of writing, scribbling, circling and underlining allows you to ingest the information, build neural pathways and to both literally and figuratively draw connections within the text.

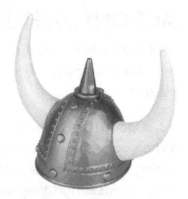

ACT ONE: WRATH OF THE VIKING

Managing The Fxxxing Viking Helmet

In Act One, we'll take a look at the Viking Helmet and examine two ways that this behaviour can manifest itself: aggressive and passive aggressive. Then we'll look at a sample scenario that illustrates the Viking Helmet in action. We'll pause so that we can provide you with a model (called the B.E.E.F. Model), that you can use to construct a challenging conversation in a constructive way. Then we will rewind the scenario and play it out again, this time using the model, so that you can see how it can be used in a real-world application. Along the way, there are a few worksheets that you can either fill out in the book or, if you don't have a pen or pencil, you can use it as a thought exercise.

ACT ONE, SCENE ONE

Let's start with one of the biggest, most striking hats that you may see employees wearing in your workplace: the Viking Helmet.

It's a good place for us to start because it's so obvious. When someone shows up at your workplace wearing a Viking Helmet, you're likely to notice. And that's the point. They're upset and they want everyone, especially you, to know it. The trick is to identify what they're upset about, because it's usually not what they say it is.

Let's start Act One, with a dialogue that looks at the Viking Helmet in action. This will give us a clear picture of how someone wearing this hat might react to a challenge on their performance. It will also give us a look at some typical pitfalls that a manager may fall prey to when reacting to this behaviour.

Lights up on Raj's office at Riverside Exploration, a mid-sized Oil Exploration Company. Véronique stands at the door to Raj's office. There's an uncomfortable silence. Finally, Véronique speaks.

VÉRONIQUE: So. I'm in trouble now?

RAJ: Hmm?

VÉRONIQUE: You said you needed to fXXXing talk to me?

RAJ: I did? Oh that! I was just blowing off steam in the lunchroom. You know how it is.

VÉRONIQUE: OK…

Silence. Raj dives in.

RAJ: But, actually, yeah, I do want to talk to you. John called me.

VÉRONIQUE: OK…

RAJ: While I was at the conference. About the status report. For the Land Continuation Obligations? The one that was due for the meeting? On Wednesday?

VÉRONIQUE (*rolls her eyes*): Oh. That.

RAJ: Yes, that.

VÉRONIQUE: Sorry about that.

RAJ: So… it won't happen again?

VÉRONIQUE: No.

RAJ: You're sure?

VÉRONIQUE: Yes.

RAJ: Because it happened this time…

VÉRONIQUE: It won't happen again!

RAJ: OK, OK. I'm just saying…

VÉRONIQUE: You're saying what?

RAJ: How do you think it's going?

VÉRONIQUE: How do you think it's going?

RAJ: I'm asking you. I want your assessment.

VÉRONIQUE: You want my assessment? It's slow, boring and tedious, that's my assessment.

RAJ: But necessary right?

Raj sits back in his chair. Véronique rolls her eyes.

RAJ: In the oil business, a company has five years from the date of leasing a property to develop it. But if a competing company begins producing nearby, then the clock starts ticking faster. It makes sense from a government point of view. They want to maximize taxable income and they don't want us squatting on a potentially good resource.

VÉRONIQUE: I've been a geologist for nine years. I know this.

RAJ: So, then you should also know that it's your job to evaluate those properties that are due to expire so we know if we need to either drill or sell. If we don't get a well drilled and producing, or sold, before the clock runs out, then the company will be stuck making unnecessary "offset obligation" payments. That will be your responsibility.

VÉRONIQUE: I got it.

RAJ: It's a hard deadline. You know that right?

VÉRONIQUE: Of course I know that.

RAJ: Then why are you spending your time on the seismic shoot with Beverly?

VÉRONIQUE: I'm not.

RAJ: Yes you are.

VÉRONIQUE: Who told you that?

RAJ: Beverly.

VÉRONIQUE (*muttering*): Bev, you stupid… She asked me to help because she's never done a shoot before.

RAJ: Yes she has.

VÉRONIQUE: Not as lead geologist.

RAJ: Well, neither have you.

VÉRONIQUE: I've been an assistant on way more than she has.

RAJ: Regardless, you're supposed to be working on the Land Continuation report.

VÉRONIQUE: It's not even my job. It's Scott's job.

RAJ: Scott's on indefinite leave.

VÉRONIQUE: When's he getting back?

RAJ: I dunno. It's indefinite.

VÉRONIQUE: Can you give me a hint?

RAJ: Look, Scott's on personal leave… I'm not supposed to… for privacy reasons I can't… Look, he's just all… from… I can't talk to you about it, OK?

VÉRONIQUE *sighs* : Fine.

RAJ: So we gotta kinda pull up our socks and get the reports done. John feels that we're behind where he wants to be. He needs the data from us by September so he can submit to the Registry.

VÉRONIQUE: Actually, John doesn't bother to submit. He hands it off to his "Land Admin Girls". And they tell me the deadline isn't until December 15th.

RAJ: Then why does John need it by
             October 1st?

VÉRONIQUE: I dunno. Cause he's a control freak
             maybe?

Raj laughs a little, and nods knowingly.

RAJ: Yeah, he kind of is. But it's his
             department and his deadline.

VÉRONIQUE: That's not the way we used to do it.
             Why is John changing things?

RAJ: All I know is, John wants it by the
             first.

VÉRONIQUE: Did he tell you why?

RAJ: No. And I don't need to know. That's
             the deadline he set, and he's got
             his reasons. Probably. Let's just get
             it done and then everybody can go
             back to getting along.

VÉRONIQUE: OK.

RAJ: OK.

Véronique starts to get up, but Raj stops her.
She slowly sits again.

RAJ: Oh! And while we're at it, please,
             please, please be sure to keep the
             progress of all those properties
             updated in the database.

Véronique rolls her eyes.

VÉRONIQUE: Really? It's just a stupid waste of time to do it all twice. Maybe if the software integrated with the data base, it would be automated, and I could be doing actual work.

RAJ: But it's not. And until it is, that's the process John wants.

VÉRONIQUE: I've tried it and it doesn't work for me.

Silence.

RAJ: So… do you need some help with that?

VÉRONIQUE: Yes.

RAJ: Well, I don't really have anyone we can spare. How behind are we?

VÉRONIQUE: The last three properties.

RAJ: I'll help you get caught up over the weekend, but after that you're on your own.

VÉRONIQUE: Oh good, then I can be working on that seismic shoot for you, which we both know is more important.

RAJ: I'm going to put Beverly on that.

VÉRONIQUE: Bev?

RAJ: She'll be fine.

VÉRONIQUE: Ya think?

RAJ: Well, if you had the land obligations finished by now…

VÉRONIQUE: Are you punishing me now? What is this, grade school?

RAJ: …and entered into the system…

VÉRONIQUE: All right I'll do it, but it's a big waste of time.

Véronique leaves. It's all she can do to not slam the door. Raj sits back, relieved that it's all over.

Evaluation

Now that you've had the opportunity to watch a Viking Helmet in action, let's analyse what we've observed.

1. How would you rate Raj's ability to deal with someone wearing a Viking Helmet?

    1   2   3   4   5   6   7   8   9   10
    Poor   Excellent

2. List three behaviours you observed in which Véronique was acting like a Viking.

    i. _____

    ii. _____

    iii. _____

3. When we work with employees who are unmanageable, or to phrase it in a more generous way, when we work with employees who have adopted behaviours that are difficult to manage, we often pass judgments. Judgments are often emotional responses masquerading as logical statements.

Without thinking too much about it, listen to your gut and list three emotions you observed in yourself that arose when Véronique was acting like a Viking.

    i. _____

    ii. _____

    iii. _____

4. If you had the opportunity to coach Véronique on her behaviour what is the single most important piece of advice you'd give her?

_____

_____

_____

5. By the end of the dialogue how likely do you think Véronique is to change?

1	2	3	4	5	6	7	8	9	10
Not Likely								Very Likely	

VIKINGS AND THEIR PROPS

When you first imagined someone in your workplace wearing a Viking Helmet, you may not have pictured someone like Véronique. You may have instinctively pictured a tall beefy Nordic man. But a person of any gender or any cultural background can wear a Viking helmet. Ours is an equal opportunity model.

You may also have thought of someone storming around the office, loudly and belligerently waving their sword and shield taking up a lot of space. You may have some people in your workplace whom you choose to give extra space to, or sit at the opposite end of a boardroom table from, or angle your chair slightly away from, or sit just a little further back from.

But a Viking doesn't need to be loud and obvious to have an impact. The individual wearing a Viking Helmet may simply take up emotional space. Their moods can be dark and cloudy, only occasionally punctuated with flashes of lightning and accompanied by crashes of thunder. In these cases, the threat of their mood is infectious and you may often find your thoughts occupied by this individual long after they've left your presence. You can often feel their mood electronically through an email or phone call. Sometimes they don't even need to be communicating with you to be exerting an influence. You could find yourself making decisions to meet their needs or anticipating their demands so you can avoid contact with them. If the result is less work for them and more for you or a counter-productive action for the company as a whole, then you may have a Viking steering the ship and you may not even realize it.

This is the less than obvious kind of Viking Helmet we find Véronique wearing. She didn't yell or threaten or push Raj around. Yet somehow by the end of the scene, he's the one who's going to be working through the weekend on the reports.

An individual wearing a Viking Helmet can take an instant dislike to a co-worker and can exhibit a hostile attitude either directly or as an aside to others. They can also take an immediate aversion towards an idea, project or proposal, as Véronique exhibited. In such cases, someone in a Viking Helmet may be outwardly hostile or they may hold up a project through deliberate procrastination or intentional mistakes.

A Viking Helmet comes with two accessories: a sword or a shield. Let's look at them one at a time.

The Viking's Sword

An employee wearing a Viking Helmet can use their sword to cut and slash their way through your company. You may hear them saying things like:

1. "I won't take on more work."
An individual wearing a Viking Helmet won't be averse to outright refusal. The sword is out and he or she is ready to use it should you dare to challenge.

2. "You can't ask me to do this."
They can use a job description as effectively as a sword. The pointy end is very useful to push back against what you're asking of them.

3. "You're being unfair."

They know the weakness in the armour of others, and fairness may be one of yours.

4. "I've tried it and it doesn't work."

Viking Helmets are often practiced in battle and have a veteran's list of war experiences to fall back upon. Any one of these stories, even the ones that have no bearing on the current situation can serve as a weapon.

5. "I'll go to the union."

An individual wearing a Viking Helmet is always ready for battle, so it's often only a short step from threats to an outright declaration of war.

These aggressive actions are frightening but at least they're easy to identify and are apparent to all. Everyone you work with sees the sword when it's drawn from its scabbard and ducks out of the way. Unfortunately, they usually cower behind you. As manager it's your job to defend your team against this internal aggressor and lay down the rule of law so that all the weapons are lowered.

Review Act One, Scene One and circle which, if any, of Véronique's lines indicated she was using her Viking sword.

The Viking's Shield

An individual wearing a Viking Helmet could also employ a shield through passive aggressive behaviour. Passive aggression is usually motivated by a person's belief that a direct expression of anger will only make their life worse but they still need to express their dissatisfaction. They end up making sarcastic comments, look at the negative consequences of any decision, or shoot down suggestions presented by others.

In fact, you're much more likely to encounter a Viking Helmet using shield behaviour than you are to see them overtly wielding a sword. So, it's worth taking a few minutes to highlight this behaviour by highlighting some common phrases that you may hear[3].

1. "Fine. Whatever."
Vikings have been known to sulk and withdraw behind their shield when they receive a direct command from the clan chieftain. Even when you spot sulking in action, the Viking Shield will sometimes deny feeling angry, even if he or she is seething on the inside. The shield is up but keep an eye on the sword arm.

2. "Sure. Let's see how long this lasts."
Sarcasm allows the Viking to use humour to covertly build allies amongst the tribe. It can also allow the Viking to appear compliant while maintaining a destructive stance. By appearing to go along, even though it's against their better

[3] Some of these come from Watson, Signe. *Ten Things Passive-Aggressive People Say: Your early-warning system for hidden hostility.* Psychology Today, posted Nov 23, 2010.

judgement, the Viking Shield can appear morally superior.

3. "You're almost pulling it off, considering your level of experience."

The backhanded compliment is another socially acceptable way for a Viking to insult someone. Often by the time you or others have realized it's an insult, the opportunity to respond has passed by.

4. "I was only joking, why are you getting so upset?"

Vikings with a shield may maintain calm and feign shock when others, worn down by his or her indirect hostility, blow up in anger. The Viking can take pleasure out of setting others up from behind the safety of the shield. It's like using the shield to inflict blunt force trauma and then apologizing for bumping into you.

5. "I'll get to it eventually."

Vikings can verbally comply with a request but delay its completion. It's like they're hiding behind the shield while making it look like they're complying. It can be used as a way of frustrating others and/or getting their way without direct conflict.

6. "It's not brain surgery."

Vikings wielding a shield may comply with a particular request, but by botching the job they get to prove their doubts were correct and blame you or others. Clever Vikings use their shield to make sure that they deflect blame for the poor performance onto you, claiming they received faulty or incomplete instructions.

7. "I thought you knew."

Claiming ignorance or choosing not to share information when it could prevent a problem, is a classic shield manoeuvre. Sometimes it results in the entire boat hitting the rocks which allows the Viking to point to your mistaken navigation as the cause.

8. "That never happened."

A Viking may use the reality distorting properties of their shield to try to convince you and others that the problem never really happened. Or if it did, it wasn't as bad as you're making it out to be. Commonly called gaslighting, it's a form of psychological manipulation that sows seeds of doubt which makes others question their own memory, perception, or even their own sanity.

Review Act One, Scene One and circle which of Véronique's lines indicated she was using her Viking shield.

Recognizing A Viking Helmet In Your Workplace

Having read the overview of an individual wearing a Viking Helmet, take some time now to reflect on your own workplace. Think about your own team or, if you don't have a team, consider your co-workers or a group you've worked with previously. Do you have (or have you had) an individual wearing a Viking Hat on your team? Do you have more than one?

1. What behaviours do you see this person demonstrating that would indicate they are wearing a Viking Helmet?

1._____

2._____

3._____

Which of the above are wielding a sword? Which are using a shield?

2. What phrases do you hear this person saying that would indicate they are wearing a Viking Helmet?

1._____

2._____

3._____

3. What impact does their behaviour have on others in the workplace?

1._____

2._____

3._____

4. On a scale of 1–10 how serious is this?

1   2   3   4   5   6   7   8   9   10

Not Serious   Very Serious

Identifying sword and shield behaviour is helpful because it reminds us that a person wearing a Viking Helmet is never unarmed. Just because the sword has been put away, doesn't mean that a shield isn't equally dangerous. The key defining factor for a Viking Helmet, whether the behaviour is aggressive or passive aggressive, is that this individual is ready to react negatively at any provocation.

Their response is perhaps the most negative that you'll encounter, so we call this a **No – (No Negative)**.

The default position of many managers is that employees wearing Viking Helmets are resistant to change because they're lazy. That's the underlying assumption behind Raj's statement, "We gotta pull up our socks and get the reports done." Labelling someone as lazy, in turn labels them as selfish, avoidant and destructive. It's hard to deal rationally, patiently and empathetically with people whom you feel are out to sabotage the company or are out to make your life miserable.

This is why it's so dangerous to confuse the person with the behaviour.

Plus, it's just plain wrong. Laziness doesn't make people lash out. It makes them check out. What we perceive as laziness usually has its roots in a deep and resentful perspective on change.

Throughout history, Vikings (and here we mean actual Norsemen) have reacted poorly to change they felt was forced upon them. For centuries the Norse thrived by using a very specific "business model" of marauding and pillaging, and built a cultural and religious structure to support those activities. As agriculture and Christianity made its way north, their culture began to change and not all of them were happy about it. Let's take a moment to observe how one historical Viking in particular, reacted poorly to feeling that change was being forced upon them.

THE OLD GODS ARE DEAD

*Harald gazed over the grey mists and icy waters, one hand resting on the hilt of his sword and the other on the carved dragon's head. His Norse longship cut through the still waters of the English river, as proud as a dragon. As proud as its warrior-king. "Thus it begins," Harald thought. "Finally, we can throw out this new god and restore the old gods to their rightful F**xxx**ing place."*

Harald was the last of the great Vikings and he knew it. He had watched his countrymen embrace the new ways of agriculture and abandon the seas that had won their forbearers such renown. With this new life came a new hierarchy. An unwelcome re-org, in which these swordsmen-turned-farmers were beholden to Earls, Dukes and Lords. Harald thought this an affront to the old ways. Long ago, in the days of Harald's father's father's father, Norsemen were equal and shared in the booty.

Harald remembered the voice of his father's father's father. The ancient one-eyed veteran stared into the fire and disdainfully proclaimed, "This is not the way we used to do things." Sitting at his feet as a lad, Harald learned that in the olden days, real men went raiding in Scotland, Ireland and England. "That's how these FXXXing Dukes and Earls should earn status," Harald thought scornfully. "Not by inheriting farmland from their father's father's father." Erik The Red didn't take an inheritance from his father, did he? No! He murdered a man, was banished from Norway and founded Greenland. That's how promotions should be handed out.

Through the mists, Harald spied a building topped with a

cross. The symbol he most despised. No wonder his people had turned soft now that they had adopted this new religion with its God of Peace. How were warriors to be inspired by two sticks tied loosely together? Harald trembled with rage when he thought of the Pope in his corner office. Why just last week, Harald got a papal newsletter explaining how The Norse should restructure. He chose to ignore these strategic plans. He dragged them to the trash without reading them.

Now he was to have England. With England under his thumb, Harald would restore his people, and their old gods, to their former glory.

The individual wearing a Viking Helmet is usually defending a certain pattern or status quo that is precious to them. Like King Harald, the modern employee is clinging to old gods and to an old way of doing things that is out-dated. The new ways confuse them and cause them to lash out.

The employee wearing the Viking Helmet is certain that the old ways of doing things are not only better, they are more virtuous. Harald is convinced that the new way of doing things is not just bad for him, it's bad for society. His modern-day counterpart, Véronique, is equally certain that Raj and John and men of their ilk are wasting everyone's time. This is no mere intellectual exercise for Véronique. She's got the experience to back it up because she proclaims, "I've tried it and it doesn't work for me". Plus, she states, "I could be working on that seismic shoot for you, which we both know is more important." In her view, it's actually dangerous and bad for the financial fortunes of the company, if she follows orders. Wearing a Viking Helmet will cause someone to think, *change is a bad idea, it's never going to work, and if I resist then I've saved everyone a ton of grief. Really, everyone who works here should be thanking me for wearing my Viking Helmet.*

But history shows us otherwise. Harald, the last Viking King, was a real person. He encountered some initial successes, including conquering the City of York. However, the better organized English forces ambushed him. Enraged, Harald worked himself into a state of berserkergang and fought aggressively. History describes him swinging his sword with both hands and hacking blindly at his foes until an arrow pierced Harald's throat and killed him. The rest of his men fled. Only 30 out of the 300 Norse ships returned home to Norway.

But the English victory was short-lived. William The Conqueror, Duke of Normandy, invaded the island three weeks later. The English forces, having marched north to defeat Harald, had to turn around and march all the way to the south coast to fight William at Hastings. The exhausted soldiers, despite fighting valiantly, were in no shape to withstand the larger army. William's descendants ruled England for the next 100 years. Their rule entrenched the hierarchical structure of nobility that Harald so despised.

Basically, Harald's refusal to adapt to change lead to the destruction not just of his company, but of the entire economy too. His dream of reversing the re-organization died with him.

This is the fate of your organization, if you let those wearing Viking Helmets, drive the ship.

Evaluating Your Own Viking Helmet

Was Raj really blameless in Act One, Scene One? Skim the dialogue again and see if you agree that maybe, just maybe, Raj was wearing a Viking Helmet of his own at some points. A leader must be aware of their own state of mind, because two Vikings clashing is never a good thing. Would you be willing to turn the lens on yourself for a moment?

1. Has there ever been an occasion when you have worn a Viking Helmet, even if it was only temporary?

_____

_____

_____

2. Remember a Viking is afraid of change and is lashing out because the old gods are dead or dying. What were your old gods that were passing away?

_____

_____

_____

3. If you had the opportunity to go back in time and coach your old boss on how to call you out on your behaviour, what is the one piece of advice you'd give her/him?

_____

_____

_____

Remember a person wearing a Viking Helmet is clinging to old gods not realizing they're already dead. Whenever you utter phrases like, "I've tried it and it doesn't work" or "That's not the way we've done it in the past", you know you're wearing a Viking Helmet.

WHERE'S THE

An elderly woman stands at a fast food counter, peering over her half-moon spectacles at a very big hamburger bun. A second elderly lady looks over her shoulder. A third, Clara wears a confused expression. On the wall behind them a poster proclaims that this is the "Home of the Big Bun." Clara leans over the counter and shouts to the invisible staff, "WHERE'S THE BEEF?"

Ken was a teenager in 1984 when Clara Peller became a spokesperson for the fast food chain, Wendy's. Clara and this catchphrase overtook the public imagination until, in what seemed like no time at all, the phrase referred to everything in our teenaged world that was substandard, half-baked or wasn't fleshed out enough. To this day it retains a citation in the McGraw-Hill Dictionary of American Idioms and Phrasal Verbs which says, "Where's the beef?" means "Where is the important content?"

In this book we'll give you a simple tool that allows you to add substance and important content to otherwise volatile conversations. For our purposes, B.E.E.F. is an acronym that stands for Behaviour, Example, Effect, Future. We'll use this simple mnemonic device, to show how to structure a challenging conversation so that your employee successfully hears the issues you have with their performance. First, you'll Identify the difficult **behaviour** and tell your employee exactly what the problem conduct is. Then you'll offer two or three specific **examples** of their behaviour. You'll want to return the conversation as often as possible to the **effect** that the employee's actions have. Once the employee has accepted that there is a problem with an effect on others, then it's time to offer help in co-creating a **future** plan of action.

Argh! There's Someone In A Viking Helmet At My Door

The advantage of the B.E.E.F Model is that it's so intuitive you can adopt it right away. You don't need to read on.

Suppose that you're about to be visited by an unmanageable employee five minutes from now. You could conceivably take out a pencil and complete the worksheet on the following page right now with no further training. Address each of the four fields in the following way:

- **Behaviour:** Identify the difficult behaviour and jot down a few notes so you can tell your seemingly unmanageable employee exactly what the problem conduct is.
- **Example:** Offer your unmanageable employee two or three specific examples of their behaviour.
- **Effect:** Return the conversation as often as possible to the effect that the employee's actions have.
- **Future:** Once the employee has accepted that there is a problem with an effect on others, then it's time for them to look for help in co-creating a future plan of action.

We'd like to think that you'd discover that your conversation would be vastly more focused and productive.

Once you finish your conversation you can return to the book and compare our detailed breakdown of the B.E.E.F. Model with your own course of action. You can compare your experience with those of our fictional characters in Act One and Two, (which have in turn been based on dozens of dialogues that have taken place in our workshops.) Watching the B.E.E.F Model applied to a number of scenarios, might expand your thinking and prompt you to apply this model to multiple circumstances.

MANAGING THE UNMANAGEABLE

BEHAVIOUR
What happened?

_____
_____
_____

EXAMPLE
Be specific.

_____
_____
_____

EFFECT
How it affects the team.

_____
_____
_____

FUTURE
What they can change.

_____
_____
_____

Behaviour

Tell your employee exactly what the difficult *behaviour* is.

This may seem self-evident, but it's surprising how often we skip this step. It's a bit like playing Charades or Pictionary; what you're trying to say seems so obvious, it's impossible to understand why everyone can't grasp it.

A failure of a leader to clearly define the problem behaviour may also be the result of a conscious or subconscious distaste for the conversation itself. In these instances, we can convince ourselves that a few sentences alluding in the vague direction of the difficulty, will crystalize the issue and we can get this unpleasantness over with quickly and go back to being buddies again. We saw Raj doing this in the example in Act One, in which he ambiguously indicated that Véronique needed to "pull up her socks".

If the manager is stressed and uneasy about addressing the subject, others will immediately have a sense that something is up. It's common practice to set the stage by asking about family, weather or weekend activities. On occasion, we may find valuable clues in responses about an issue in the subject's personal life, but the deep issues are unlikely to spill out unexpectedly, while speculating on the possibility of rain or the outcome of an under 14 soccer match. When tensions are already high, this is only delaying the inevitable. While remaining empathetic is necessary, it's best to dive in early. Camaraderie can be established by brainstorming solutions once the elephant in the room has been named.

An employee, particularly a Viking Helmet or a Sun Hat, may be aware that there is a problem but may be in denial. Remember that this may be the first time that anyone has pointed out to them that this behaviour is inappropriate. In some cases, it may take time for this new information to sink in. You can help them out by introducing the problem with a very clear statement and being as specific as possible about what the behaviour is.

In cases with multiple concerns that you wish to address, select the most important issue and deal with that, reserving the other matters for follow up conversations. Otherwise, you may find yourself beginning the conversation with a laundry list of complaints. This can be overwhelming and can shut your team member down, before the conversation can even begin. Trying to find a solution or suggest ways to modify conduct with someone who is simply not listening, is an uphill battle.

What's The Problem Behaviour?

If you can't get away from the laundry list, or if there are so many problems that you can't figure out where to start, write a list of the multiple problem incidents beforehand, using the worksheet on the next page.

- Write as many problem behaviours as you can think of in each circle. Use only one or two words, at most three. Don't elaborate. That'll just get you even more frustrated.

- Write out all the examples you can think of. Don't edit at this stage. Just dump your grievances on the page.

- Got it all out? Good. Because you're not going to take that anger into the meeting with you.

- Ask yourself, *if they could change one thing that would have the greatest impact on them, on me and everyone else, what would that be?*

- Place it in the centre of the worksheet.

KEEP THIS PAGE HANDY

Keep this page handy. After you address this central problem behaviour, you're going to return to this page in the coming weeks and start working on the other issues. That way you know that the problems won't be later forgotten (or glossed over with a sigh of relief once you see minor progress.)

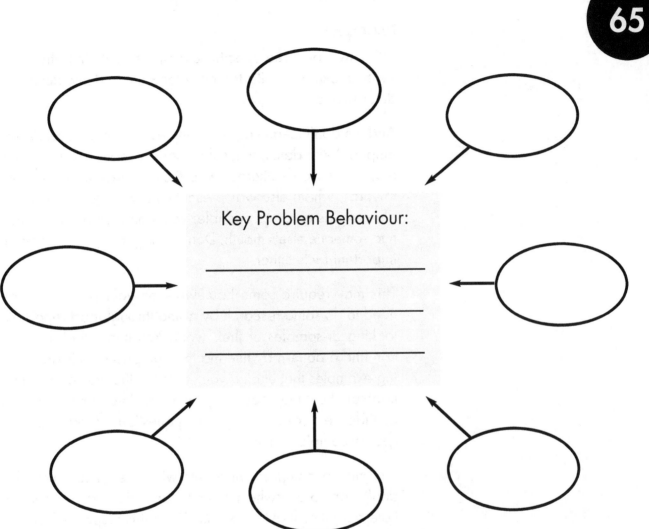

Key Problem Behaviour:

_____

_____

_____

If they could change one thing that would have the greatest impact on them, on me and everyone else, what would that be? Rewrite that behaviour in the centre.

Examples

Offer two or three specific *examples* of their behaviour. Without examples, it's too easy for them to deny, deflect or defer blame.

And we don't mean vague examples. We mean *specific* examples. With dates, times, locations, actions taken or omitted, exact words uttered, who those words were directed towards, whom else was present as a witness. Avoid paraphrasing as much as possible; you'll only be putting words into someone else's mouth. Don't exaggerate, but don't omit important facts either.

This may require some homework on your part. You may need to do some research by going through past reports or looking at samples of their work. You might find that you can find a pattern by filtering through past emails and finding examples that eluded you earlier or that you didn't highlight at the time. You may want to interview others in confidence or ask subtle probing questions of teammates to get the complete picture.

You must accomplish all of this while being succinct. You don't want to overwhelm your conversation partner and initiate a fight or flight response. Once this response kicks in, it becomes increasingly difficult to move the conversation forward. Use examples for an altruistic goal; helping them improve at their work. This is a substantial paradigm shift away from using examples to reprimand an employee.

Effect

Return the conversation as often as possible to the *effect* that the employee's actions have had. This is perhaps the most powerful element of the B.E.E.F. Model, because it provides you with an opportunity to make the past consequences of their behaviour crystal clear. Until this point, they are likely to dispute the behaviour you're talking about by saying something along the lines of "that never happened." They may also debate the examples you've provided, "Well, it happened, but it didn't happen that way." Even if you've convinced them of what they're doing and when it happened, there is still room for them to minimize the impact of their actions.

You can shape the effect by looking at any one, or all, of the following:

> **The impact on the company.** Actual dollars and cents are concrete and objective, and you'd think they'd be difficult to argue with. As leaders, we tend to default to building an argument that centres on the impact on the company because it seems rational and therefore should be effective. It would be, if we were dealing with creatures of pure logic, like Mr Spock on *Star Trek*. Spock and his fellow Vulcans long ago abandoned emotion and made every decision based on cold hard logic. However, you're not dealing with Vulcans, you're dealing with humans. Just like Spock and *Star Trek*, the idea that you can convince anyone

to do anything using logic is fiction. Emotions are a vital part of our decision-making process, even when we are not conscious of them.

Your employee has an emotional connection to their current behaviour so it is easy for them to use logic against you and rationalize their actions. They may dismiss your description of the effect on the company by saying or thinking, *a single mistake isn't going to sink the company.* Or *these are special circumstances that require an exception this time.* Or even, *you're just overreacting and being emotional.*

While it's important to outline the impact that your employee's behaviour has on the company, you can't stop there.

The effect on themselves. Outlining the effects an individual's behaviour is having on themselves, is often a sobering argument. For some employees, this is more effective because we are all hardwired to look out for ourselves. You may not be in a position to threaten someone with termination or performance improvement measures but pointing out how their current behaviour is going to appear on their performance review, can motivate them to change.

You could also describe the effect on their status. Some employees are seeking attention from others, trying to gather allies amongst the team members or even just following another charismatic problem employee. Pointing out that this behaviour is having the opposite effect on their social status within the company can lead to change.

Some team members identify closely with a project, tool they've developed or program they've created. They may see it as an extension of themselves. Identifying how their behaviour is causing damage to a project, tool or program that they are proud of can have a very similar effect as describing the effect on their personal status.

The effect on others. This is perhaps the most powerful way to express the effect because it works on both a strategic and an emotional level. Strategically, it's hard to muster a counterargument when you have evidence of specific effects their behaviour has on others in the team. For instance, it's easier for an employee to claim that he is late because he is a victim of the bus schedule. It's much harder for them to dispute that, since Johanne can't leave until he arrives, he is making it impossible for her to pick up her child from daycare on time and causing her to pay extra fees in unnecessary overtime care. That is an effect for which you have witnesses and you can gather supporting evidence such as daycare receipts.

The second reason stating the effect that their behaviour has on others is effective is emotional. Most everyone has a basic desire to be accepted, liked and acknowledged by their team members. We are descendants of people who thrived in tribes, villages or small communities, so we are hard-wired to perceive relatedness as essential to survival. In a modern workplace this hardwiring means that the majority of people more or less want to get along with their colleagues[4].

Avoid a reference to emotion at this stage, especially the emotions of others who are not present. For example, "You offended Beth when you made that comment." This allows the employee to debate the impact of the comment and Beth's reaction. This kind of comment is likely to be met with "Well, she never said anything about it to me."

The truth is that it may take all three of these ways of looking at the effect to achieve the impact you're looking for. Amongst psychologists, the jury is still out on whether humans are innately altruistic or selfish. Numerous studies have proven both are correct at various times, which simply indicates that people are different. Some are motivated by self-preservation, some by a desire to be accepted by their peers and some by an appeal to a larger sense of purpose. It may be necessary to try all three methods in tandem.

[4] With a few exceptions. As we stated earlier, if you're dealing with someone who genuinely takes pleasure in making life difficult for their co-workers, for you and/or for the company in general, then you're likely not dealing with a challenging employee, but a sociopathic one. That moves beyond the scope of this book and we happily refer you to resources at the end of this book.

Future

Your work is not yet over, even though your employee understands there is a problem, has understood the examples and is clear on the effect. There is an understandable tendency to wipe your brow with relief, sink back in your chair and try to get back to normal. Without the next step, you're doomed to repeat this cycle over again.

You must close with a discussion of *future* actions that can be taken to correct the behaviour.

Encourage them to continue to take ownership of the problem. It may be tempting to remove them from the situation, to ask others to change their behaviour or to change the structure to accommodate them. Make sure that the solutions are about *them* changing *their* behaviour[5].

It's important to make sure that they understand that there is a way for them to change. If they come to think that there is no solution, then they may be in danger of reverting to their Viking Helmet just when you've convinced them to remove it.

Worse yet, if they come to think there is something wrong with them as a person, then there is no possibility for them to change, and they might as well continue with their behaviour, since it's inevitable anyway. This is where thinking of the behaviour as a hat comes in handy.

Finally, before drawing the conversation to a close, reinforce that there is an expectation of accountability. They are expected to follow the plan you've co-created, and you must make it clear that you will be following up with them. Then

[5] This statement assumes that the problem is not a reaction to an issue of safety, abuse or a disrespectful workplace. Unfortunately, it sometimes happens that an individual who is demonstrating undesirable behaviour, is responding to protect themselves. Their reactions may be inappropriate but if they're putting on a Viking Helmet to protect themselves from others, then you have a different problem on your hands than you expected. If your challenge conversation has uncovered this circumstance, then you may need to pause and conduct more investigations. It may even be that you need to have a challenge conversation with a different Viking.

of course, you actually have to follow up. You cannot risk being perceived as a manager who makes false threats, who doesn't follow through and who doesn't hold them accountable. You might as well just hand them their Viking Helmet and a chin strap to make sure it never comes off. In accountable organizations, no one should expect to "stay under the radar", including yourself.

At all stages of this conversation, it's important to remember that it's not about punishment, it's about improvement. Using the B.E.E.F. Model allows you to use the conversation to identify a specific problem related to performance and not attack them as individuals in a way that threatens their self-worth. As a result, you are much more likely to be able to position the conversation so that you gain their commitment to address a problem. In short, handled correctly, you can get the employee to identify ways they can correct the problem themselves, so that they do the heavy lifting for you.

ACT ONE, SCENE TWO

Let's pay a return visit to Riverside Exploration and see if applying the B.E.E.F. Model to the conversation can help Raj get more effective results from his conversation with Véronique.

Raj closes the door to his office firmly. He knows his assistant is eager to ask him a few questions, but he also knows that he needs a few minutes to focus his attention on his upcoming conversation.

He rubs his eyes vigorously trying to focus and begins searching. "Where is that worksheet?", he mutters to himself. He knows he should have gone to bed as soon as he returned home from the airport, but he also doesn't regret the late-night conversation he had with his wife, because it helped prepare him for this morning. It was his wife that helped Raj recall that Véronique had not always been a problem. In fact, when she was first transferred to his department, Raj had told her Véronique was a welcome addition to the team.

It was also his wife who reminded him of the course on effective communication he had signed himself up for a few months ago. Raj had recognized that years in the engineering trade, had left him weak on the soft skills. Now that he was spending more and more of his time managing people and not well sites, he needed some sort of system to structure the conversations. The course had seemed like a good idea. One thing that had stuck with him from that course was a simple but effective template.

Raj suppresses a shout of excitement and gives a silent prayer of thanks to the office gods. It had only taken him a minute and a half to find the worksheet. Four minutes left. Raj glances at the worksheet: Behaviour, Examples, Effects and Future. Seems simple enough.

Raj is halfway through the worksheet when the phone rings. He's about to ignore it when he instinctively looks at the name on the call display. John. Again. He doesn't have time for John and his habit of endlessly repeating the same refrain, but...

Raj answers the phone.

"Hi John, I only have a second, because Véronique is going to be here any moment but I have to ask you a question."

Lights up. Raj is on the phone. He sees Véronique lingering at the door and, using hand gestures, he asks her to hold on for a moment.

RAJ: OK. I gotta go. I said gotta go.

Raj hangs up, opens the door and turns his complete attention to Véronique.

VÉRONIQUE: You wanted to see me?

RAJ: I do. I need to talk you about where we're at with the Land Continuation Obligations.

VÉRONIQUE: Oh that.

RAJ: John and I were looking at the latest status updates in the system, and I can see that to date, you've only submitted two out of ten to him.

VÉRONIQUE: Yeah, but three more are nearly finished.

RAJ: OK, that's good to know. John didn't know that, and he had a meeting with the CEO. You haven't been keeping the status updated in the system here, so as far as John can see, nothing's moving forward. So, what happens is, John calls me when I'm down at the conference and I can't see where things are at in the system either, so I look like I don't know what my team members are up to. Then I call you. And here we are.

VÉRONIQUE: OK. I get it.

RAJ: So?

VÉRONIQUE: So, I'll update the database.

RAJ: I appreciate that. Let's recap so I can get a clear picture of where we're at. Is that OK?

VÉRONIQUE: Sure.

RAJ: Two have been submitted to John and his team, three more are coming. And we've agreed you're going to update the database. What's up with the other five?

VÉRONIQUE: They're coming.

RAJ: I see that John set a deadline of September 1st for all ten.

VÉRONIQUE: Actually, John doesn't bother to submit them. He hands it off to his "Land Admin Girls". And they tell me the deadline isn't until December 15th.

RAJ: John wants it by the first -

VÉRONIQUE: Did he tell you why?

RAJ: Actually, he did. Well, not at first, I had to go back and ask him. That's why I was still on the phone when you came in. John and his team are trying to be really proactive this year. It seems that a few years ago we had a lease on a property up by Penhold and Shell started drilling on land immediately adjacent. Do you remember this?

VÉRONIQUE: Sort of...

RAJ: So that meant that Riverside had eighteen months to either drill on the land or make a case as to why we weren't producing. Otherwise...

VÉRONIQUE: Otherwise we have to pay obligation royalties to the government. I know how it works.

RAJ: But here's the thing; no one noticed until the expiry came up. John's team had to scramble to make a case, and even then, they were six months late. So, the company had to pay fines for six months - no - nine months, by the time the submission went through. AND, to top it all off, last month they decided the play wasn't even worth the risk and they let it expire anyway. That's a lot of money out the door in obligation penalties on land we don't even want and during a recession. That's the equivalent of one person's salary. We laid off five people about that same time. Maybe if we hadn't wasted all that money on offset obligation penalties, we could have saved at least one of those jobs. You see where I'm going with this.

VÉRONIQUE: I'm not stupid Raj.

RAJ: No one's saying you are. I just want to be clear that there are consequences. No, sorry, "consequences" makes it sound too harsh. Effects. I'm saying there are knock-on effects. When you don't update the system, John's left in the dark, I look like an idiot, the company loses money and jobs might be lost. The more important effect is that if you don't get these to John by the first, then his team doesn't have the time to evaluate which lands are worth keeping and which aren't.

VÉRONIQUE: John needs four months to figure that out?

RAJ: He might be over-compensating.

VÉRONIQUE: Might?

RAJ: OK, between you and me he IS over-compensating. But you can hardly blame him when he got burned so bad in the past. And if we don't hold up our end, then John doesn't have the chance to refine his new workflow. Besides, we don't know what else he may have on his plate in December. Apart from the fact that we lose nearly two weeks for holidays, not to mention office Christmas celebrations and all that, he may have a bunch of other hard deadlines all at once.

VÉRONIQUE: I got it.

RAJ: I know you do. I just want to be clear.

Raj stands, Veronique heads for the door. Raj raises a hand to stop her.

So, moving forward what are we going to do?

VÉRONIQUE: Get five more done by October 1st.

RAJ: And?

VÉRONIQUE: Update the database on the other three.

RAJ: Thanks. Let's check in next week and see how it's going, OK?

Veronique exits.

Evaluation

Now that you've had the opportunity to watch the B.E.E.F. Model in action, let's analyze what we've observed.

1. Re-read Take Two just looking at Raj's lines. Mark out the sections where Raj is:

- Speaking about Véronique's BEHAVIOUR.
- Providing EXAMPLES of her behaviour.
- Identifying the EFFECTS of her behaviour.
- Requesting different behaviour in the FUTURE.

Please feel free to write in the book.

2. Now re-read the same dialogue, but this time just looking at Véronique's lines.

- Draw a pair of horns beside those moments where Véronique puts on her Viking Helmet.
- Observe the strategies Raj employs to defuse the behaviour.

3. Do you feel that Véronique understands and has accepted that there is an issue with her behaviour?

☐ Yes

☐ No

4. On a scale of 1 to 10 how likely do you think Véronique is to remove her Viking Helmet and change her behaviour in the future?

1	2	3	4	5	6	7	8	9	10
Not Likely									Very Likely

Where was the B.E.E.F.?

In our experience what makes the B.E.E.F. Model so effective is its simplicity. By "simple" we don't mean dumbed-down or reductive. Simple means that an idea is sticky, can be easily recalled and quickly applied even under pressure and when the stakes are high. For example, Raj was able to apply the B.E.E.F. Model immediately once he'd found the worksheet. He was quickly able to identify at least two behaviours that he wanted to address, to make note of specific examples and to identify the effects. He hadn't yet finished when the phone rang.

Significantly, Raj gave himself the time he needed to focus his thoughts and marshal his energy before Véronique arrived. As David Rock notes in his book *Your Brain at Work*, "The big problem with distractions, whether internal or external, is that they are, well, distracting. One theory about why this is the case is that over millions of years, your brain learned to orient attention to anything unusual[6]." Or, as scientist and philosopher Jonathan Haidt at the University of Virginia says, "We are the descendants of people who paid a lot of attention when there was a rustle in the bushes." This tendency to be distracted that once kept your ancestors alive long enough to create you, is a liability in a world where you are encouraged to always be on. Taking a moment to clear the stage was especially important for Raj because he knew difficult conversations were one of his weak spots.

Before the conversation began, Raj made an important, if subconscious, paradigm shift by acknowledging that Véronique was not a bad person and that she had been pro-

[6] If you're looking for more, this quote can be found on page 50 of *Your Brain at Work: Strategies for Overcoming Distraction, Regaining Focus, and Working Smarter All Day Long* by David Rock.

ductive in the past. Focusing on the behaviour and not the person, helped Raj no longer feel obligated to be everybody's friend. He was not talking about her. Instead he was talking about her actions.

This shift not only makes for an easier conversation for Raj, it also makes it easier for Véronique. By focusing on her behaviour and by using specific examples, the entire conversation is less personal and thus she has less justifiable reason to get upset. Véronique can't very well argue that John wasn't left in the dark, because he clearly was when he went into the meeting armed with inaccurate or out-of-date information. Though Véronique was still wearing her Viking Helmet, in Take Two, she was much less defensive. It's as if she was wearing her helmet, but she had few opportunities to use it. It's significant to note that when we change the way we think about others, we significantly change the way they react to us.

All of this happened despite the fact that Raj was more pointed and blunt in his comments. In Act One, Scene One, Raj was not specific; he beat around the bush before getting to the point and he even punished Véronique by assigning Bev the important work that Véronique was sneaking off to do. In Act One, Scene Two, Raj is direct about why the meeting is taking place ("I need to talk to you about where we're at with the Land Continuation Obligations"). He is blunt with his examples ("You haven't been keeping the status of those updated in the system"). And he pulls no punches when outlining the effects of her actions ("When you don't update the system, John's left in the dark, I look like an idiot, the company loses money and jobs might be lost".) She might have quibbled about the degree of impact, or the extent to which John or Raj over-reacted, but even if she had, the effect remains. John's opinion was that he was hung out to dry and Raj felt that he looked like he didn't know what his team members were up to and there was potential for negative consequences for the company that could result in job losses.

Often when we approach these difficult conversations, we begin by being timid and we phrase our comments with extra care. But as we've seen here, if one takes the time to clearly separate the behaviour from the individual, then there's less opportunity for both parties to get aggressive or defensive.

Despite his decision to ignore distractions by focusing his attention, Raj was wise to accept John's call at the last minute, because it afforded him the opportunity to get further information. This paid off when Véronique started trying to downplay the importance of the deadline. Contrast this with Act One, Scene One, when Raj said that he didn't know why John was changing the way things are done ("I don't need to know. That's the deadline he set, and he's got his reasons. Probably").

This is a lesson to us all; it's important to complete sufficient research to be able to state the effects clearly. Imagine if Raj had exaggerated the effects or the impact it had had on John or on him. Maybe you've been in a situation where a boss has shouted, "You've ruined my career!" Like me, you'd probably roll your eyes at that one. Employing such hyperbole undermines one's credibility. Even when Véronique claims he's over-reacting, Raj admits candidly that John might be over-compensating, but he goes on to credit John with having a good reason. He further notes that it is their responsibility to help John out with his new workflow by completing their responsibilities and meeting his requested deadline.

As intimidating as a person wearing a Viking Helmet can be, it's easy behaviour to identify. And as intimidating as it is to confront, you know you've got to do it. It's much harder to identify an employee who is wearing a Sun Hat and it's not always easy to figure out which conversation techniques will get through to them and create a change in behaviour. In Act Two, we'll look at the Sun Hat and at an example from the public sector of a manager who must have a challenging conversation with someone who'd rather be on the beach or drinking a Mai Tai in the bar.

Put What You've Learned Into Practice

Consider the team members you described in the worksheet entitled "Recognizing Viking Helmet Wearers" earlier in Act One, which invited you to identify one or more individuals wearing a Viking Helmet in your workplace.

Write down three specific actions you could take, starting tomorrow to address their behaviour.

1. _____

_____

_____

2. _____

_____

_____

3. _____

_____

_____

SUMMARY

The individual wearing a Viking Helmet takes up a lot of emotional space and you may find yourself avoiding dealing with them because it's so intimidating.

Employees wearing a Viking Helmet can be grouped into two broad categories:

- The Viking Helmet with a sword is overtly aggressive.
- The Viking Helmet with a shield is passive aggressive.

The default position of many managers is that employees wearing Viking Helmets are resistant to change because they're lazy. But laziness doesn't make people lash out. It makes them check out. What we perceive as laziness usually has it's roots in a nostalgia for the way things were and a resentment to change. We've nicknamed this "worshiping the old gods."

The B.E.E.F. Model is a useful tool to structure a conversation. It consists of four steps:

- **Behaviour:** Identify the difficult *behaviour* and jot down a few notes so you can tell your seemingly unmanageable employee exactly what is the problem conduct.
- **Example:** Offer your unmanageable employee two or three *specific examples* of their behaviour.
- **Effect:** Return the conversation as often as possible to the *effect* that the employee's actions have on others.
- **Future:** Once the employee has accepted that there is a problem with an effect on others, then it's time for them look for help in co-creating a *future* plan of action.

The advantage of this model is that you can implement it right away.

ACT TWO: IF IT AIN'T BROKE DON'T FIX IT

Managing The Fxxxing Sun Hat

In Act Two, we'll take a look at the Sun Hat and examine two ways that this behaviour can manifest itself: disengaged and critical. Then we'll look at a sample scenario that illustrates the Sun Hat in action. As before, we will rewind the scenario and play it out again, using the B.E.E.F. Model, so that you can see how it can be used in a real-world application. This time we'll look at a third scene that examines the consequences of not being clear on next steps. Along the way, there are a few worksheets that you can either fill out in the book or, if you don't have a pen or pencil, you can use as a thought exercise. To begin with, we'll turn to a historical incident to point out the impact a negative Sun Hat can have on vulnerable co-workers.

TAKE THE CARPENTER WITH YOU

Chippy stood on the frozen beach facing his team lead, who was telling him and his twenty-six co-workers that the business plan was a failure and they were all doomed to a cold and hungry death. The team leader, Ernest, was trying to put a good face on a difficult situation with a compelling presentation. Six of them would be promoted to a special project, he said. The special project consisted of sailing away to civilization and leaving the majority behind to survive a third winter without enough resources to do the job properly.

*"F**xxx** this," Chippy thought.*

Chippy remembered the job advert Ernest had placed in the London Times. "Men wanted for hazardous journey. Low wages, bitter cold, long hours of complete darkness. Safe return doubtful. Honour and recognition in event of success."

Now, after 455 days trapped on the ice, Chippy felt bitter and disengaged from the business strategy. He hadn't always been. On the southward voyage, Chippy responded with ever more innovative solutions as the conditions worsened. He erected a set of windscreens to protect the helmsman from the fierce polar winds. When the ice grew so thick it threatened to choke the propeller, he built a small stage over the stern to allow a sailor to keep it clear of the heavy ice. Even when the ship began to be crushed by the ice, Chippy was caulking holes in the hull with strips of ripped blankets soaked in a mixture of seal blood and flour while standing knee deep in freezing water for hours at a time.

No one had been more dedicated than he, but once the ship was well and truly lost, Chippy gave up all hope.

"We must leave this barren place in the only lifeboat left to us." Ernest announced to the rag-tag crew arrayed in front of him. "Tomorrow we sail to the Whaling Station on South Georgia Island."

"Tha' madness!" Chippy thought to himself and stretched out on the rocks. "Our leader has nae got a solid turn-around plan for leadin` us out o' this mess."

"There's room for only six of us. Myself, Worsley, John, Timothy, Tom…" Ernest paused. He took a deep breath. "… and Chippy."

"Me?" Chippy exclaimed, astonished.

"We'll need provisions for 4 weeks."

"We'd best take a little more," Chippy piped up.

"If we haven't made landfall in four weeks we won't be making it all. No sense wasting food."

The men dispersed. But before Chippy could drag himself to his feet, he was stopped by the expedition's team leader.

"I need to F**xxx**ing talk to you," said Ernest. "You haven't been meeting your KPIs. And your attitude is deplorable."

"If I'm such a pain in th' bahookie, then how come yer takin' me alang?"

"Because if I leave you here, all twenty-two men left behind will die. That's the effect you have on others."

A heavy silence filled the biting air as Ernest's words sunk in. Chippy stared at the flimsy lifeboat that was to bear their special projects team to salvation.

"For the sake of all these men, you have to make this boat strong enough to sail 800 miles."

Chippy didn't take his eyes off the boat, but he heard Ernest walking away, the gravel crunching under his feet. He stared at the craft for a long time. Perhaps if he pirated some material from one of the other lifeboats, he could raise the sides enough to keep some of the seawater out.

Ernest Shackleton, Harry "Chippy" McNish and four other men accomplished one of the most daring and exceptional feats of seamanship in recorded history. Within hours of setting out, the tiny craft was weighed down by thick ice. As the weather worsened, the crew came to realize that they were in in the midst of a hurricane. They later found out that the same storm sunk a sturdy 550-ton steamer that was also trying to get to South Georgia Island. Thanks to the extended side panels that Chippy had constructed, the six-man crew successfully crossed 800 miles of open sea in a boat that Chippy repaired daily. They finally arrived, with pinpoint accuracy, on the tiny island.

However, they'd landed on the wrong side. The ravaged boat was in no condition to circumnavigate the island, so Ernest divided his crew into two parties. He left Chippy in charge of those on the beach and, with two other sailors, he walked 26 miles across the unexplored mountainous interior. Before they left, Chippy salvaged screws from the wreck which he drove through the soles of the men's boots to give them traction on the glaciers. Chippy gave Ernest 50 feet of rope and his carpenter's adze[7]. It took Ernest four attempts, over four months, in four different ships, to rescue the men he and Chippy had left behind. In the end, Ernest Shackleton rescued all twenty-two men, without a single loss of life.

At the time, Shackleton was viewed as a failure when compared to other polar explorers, but history has recognized that his understanding of how to motivate people and build morale amongst a team makes him a model leader. Chippy was a negative, unresponsive, disengaged personality, a quintessential Sun Hat, but the decision to keep the most disruptive person closest, may have saved the crew.

A Sun Hat may be unpleasant. We may be tempted to give up on them, to leave them behind because they can have a corrosive influence on other team members. What is easier for us in the short term, is rarely effective in the long run. Instead of ignoring the problem, it's vital to address it head on. If we have the bravery and courage to have a difficult workplace conversation, we may find ourselves rewarded with personal growth in our employees that can astonish and inspire all the leaders.

Before we continue, let's delve into what we mean by an employee wearing a Sun Hat.

[7] It's worth noting that the next successful crossing of South Georgia Island wasn't attempted until 1955 and only then by a much better equipped team of experienced mountaineers.

START OFF SLOW AND THEN EASE OFF

The individual wearing a Sun Hat is so disengaged they might as well be reading a trashy novel on the beach or drinking a cocktail on the patio of the local bar. They're the kind of person who begins a project with the phrase, "Start off slow and then eeeeeaase off." Those wearing Sun Hats are just as common in a contemporary workplace as those wearing a Viking Helmet, but their actions take the opposite form. Their response is not quite as negative as a Viking Helmet, so we call The Sun Hat No Positive.

A Sun Hat in the workplace might take a two-hour lunch break, make personal calls, or surf the web all day. Strategies for getting out of their own work may include over-delegating tasks to juniors or trying to delegate upwards. This is the kind of individual who comes into your cubical to gossip or pass the time, while you hustle to keep up with your daily workload. If they are truly disengaged, they may be completing their résumé or applying for other jobs while still "working" for you.

Popular culture offers us a vast array of contemporary touch points for the Sun Hat in action. One of the most popular is Wally from the syndicated Dilbert cartoons. Wally is the lazy, coffee-addicted engineer, who is highly skilled at doing no work, while avoiding punishment from the boss. He is the kind of character that proudly claims that, "I used the week to develop some new coffee sipping noises."

When an employee like Wally puts on the Sun Hat, these (in)actions are overt and relatively easy to identify as long as you catch them in the act. Unlike the Viking Helmet, an individual wearing a Sun Hat is almost always disguising or justifying their inactivity. This makes their actions difficult to challenge. To properly address this behaviour, it's useful to subdivide the Sun Hat into two broad categories. The Sun Hat on the beach and the Sun Hat in the Tiki Lounge. Let's look at each in turn.

The Sun Hat On The Beach

Laziness isn't the only manifestation of a Sun Hat individual. In fact, a person wearing a Sun Hat may be very active, like a vacationer who powers through a 500-page bestseller in a single afternoon while lounging on the beach. There's nothing lazy about that. They just don't put their effort into what you want them to.

A person wearing a Sun Hat is only active about things that engage them. For instance, if they are particularly social they may spend a lot of their workday consulting with others as they organize the staff Christmas party. Or their focus may be on formatting the newsletter for the company's Fantasy Football league. Or they may turn their attention to a task that they haven't been assigned because it interests them.

But before we pass too many judgments, we must recognize that many have no realization that there is a need to change. They may earnestly believe that the Fantasy Football League is essential to morale. Or they may think that you want them to focus on the staff Christmas party. In such cases you may hear a Sun Hat on the Beach saying things like:

1. "Sure, I'd be happy to."

A Sun Hat may seem concerned or super-polite to your face. Yet, as soon as you turn your back, they're on the beach, engrossed in the next chapter of their best-seller. Keep in mind this is not punishing behaviour; that's the domain of the Viking Helmet. The Sun Hat motivation is that they don't value the assigned work as much as their own pet projects.

2. "I didn't know you meant *now*."

Procrastination is a useful way to prolong the rest period. Sometimes stalling is a conscious activity, though it's also possible that these are subconscious behaviours, allowing them to fool themselves into spending more time on their preferred activities.

3. "I'm trying to get to it."

Sometimes they don't have a good way of organizing their work or managing their time or are easily overwhelmed. They may have slowed to a snail's pace to make sure that they don't forget anything.

4. "I'm on target, so what's the fuss?"

Experience has shown the Sun Hat that the work always gets done, eventually… by someone. He or she may not realize that the reason it gets done is because someone else comes to the rescue

5. "We've always done it this way, so if it ain't broke, don't fix it."

The old process may be time-consuming and inefficient, but it's effective. The new way of doing things will be time-consuming to learn (at least in the short-term), so the Sun Hat is quite justified in ignoring you. It's better for their workflow. Long-standing processes are outdated, but like the Sun Hat itself, it conforms to their body and is familiar. Never mind the sweat stains and smell.

6. "I've always been good at this."
And they have. That's why you hired / promoted / didn't fire them. And they've been doing it longer than you. So leave the Sun Hat alone to get on with it. Yeesh.

It's important to realize that a person wearing a Sun Hat on the beach believes what they're saying. They really do believe they are on target. They really do believe that it ain't broke. And they definitely didn't hear you say that they should change the way they do things. In short, their world-view boils down to "my present situation feels good enough as it is."

The Sun Hat in the Tiki-Bar
An individual wearing a Sun Hat may believe they are completely justified in retiring to the Tiki Bar, where they can watch in relative comfort while others do the work. Unlike the Sun Hat on the Beach, this individual is aware they're avoiding their duties and believes that this is the best course of action.

Russell has observed many unionized environments where unionized employees take every opportunity to work the system. When he spent time chatting with these individuals, he discovered that Sun Hat behaviour often stems from a belief that the company is out to screw them, so they must pre-emptively act out of self-interest to protect themselves. The Sun Hat in the Tiki Bar believes motivation is a sign of either a "sucker" who doesn't know any better or a "suck up" who wants to get ahead at their expense.

Ken's experience with unionized environments in Western Canada revealed individuals who were hopeful and even deeply engaged at one point, but were frustrated when the status quo reasserted itself, time after time. Some were the drivers of change at one point, inventing new processes and taking risks, but felt punished in some subtle way for their ingenuity. Now, as Sun Hats, they rationalize their disappointment to protect themselves. A Sun Hat is a lot like Wally, Dilbert's companion, who said, "Always remember that when you reach for the stars they're too far away, so it's hopeless."

You may find the Sun Hat in the Tiki Bar saying things like:

1. "I've tried it and it doesn't work."
This individual always knows better, because they've seen it fail in the past. They're happy for you to knock yourself out while they watch.

2. "Things are always in flux."
This person has learned that acting immediately gives higher-ups the opportunity to change their minds, provide revisions or expand the scope. It's less painful to wait until all the facts are in and then pull an all-nighter. Less painful for them anyway.

3. "I don't need help."

The Peter Principle suggests that corporations promote competent people until they are eventually in a role where they are out of their depth. You may have an employee who feels facing one's own limitations is scary. So maybe the Sun Hat will see what's up in the break room instead.

4. "No one else is doing it."

Workplace cultures often inspire groupthink. If many individuals in the same company are also wearing Sun Hats, then it can become a fashion trend.

5. "It's not on my job description."

The last refuge of the Sun Hat is to retreat into the protective cocoon of their contract. Russell's fellow Englishmen have a specific phrase for this behaviour: "jobsworth". The term is derived from the phrase, "I won't do that, it's more than my job's worth".

There are a lot of similarities between the individual wearing the Sun Hat in the Tiki Bar and a Viking Helmet wielding a shield. Both are passive aggressive but the difference lies in their motivation. The Viking Helmet is lashing out due to overt or repressed anger or frustration. The Sun Hat is almost always retreating or withdrawing out of self-interest.

Re-reading the list of statements above, you may see how this individual is rationalizing their "no". It's not in their interest to act on your instructions. In fact, it's not in anyone's interest. Really, they should be rewarded. They're saving everyone a lot of extra trouble.

There are, of course, consequences to The Sun Hat's activities (or lack thereof):

- The average worker admits to frittering away 3 hours per 8-hour workday, not including lunch and other scheduled breaks.
- 64% of workers admit to using the internet for personal purposes during work hours.
- 60% of online purchases are made during regular work hours.
- 65% of YouTube viewers watch between 9am-5pm on weekdays when (presumably) at work.
- 77% of workers who have a Facebook account use it during work hours; fully 1/3 of those ONLY use Facebook at work.
- 39% of millennials would consider quitting their jobs if Facebook were banned at work.

Clearly there is a cost to wearing a Sun Hat. The 18 hours per week that employees spend surfing the internet equals $759 Billion in total salary cost for employers.

Before you dive in and call out the individual wearing the Sun Hat, it's important to recognize that all of us are prone to wearing a Sun Hat from time to time. It may not be desirable, but it's understandable if an employee is preoccupied with a personal matter, such as a health issue or family problem. If they've been a good performer previously, then a behaviour change is a signal that something has recently changed, and it's worth investigating why they've checked out. Your job in these moments is to help them set aside the Sun Hat after a period of time and restore their Hard Hat or Graduate Cap.

Recognizing the Sun Hat in Your Workplace

Having read the overview of Sun Hat behaviour, take some time now to reflect on your own workplace. Think about your own team or, if you don't have a team, consider your co-workers or a group you've worked with previously. Do you have (or have you had) an individual wearing a Sun Hat in your team? Do you have more than one?

1. What behaviours do you see this person demonstrating that would indicate they are wearing a Sun Hat?

1. _____
2. _____
3. _____

Which of the above are on the beach? Which are in the Tiki Bar?

2. What phrases do you hear this person saying that would indicate they are wearing a Sun Hat?

1. _____
2. _____
3. _____

3. What impact does their behaviour have on others in the workplace?

1. _____
2. _____
3. _____

4) On a scale of 1-10 how serious is this?

1   2   3   4   5   6   7   8   9   10

Not Serious   Very Serious

ACT TWO, SCENE ONE

Let's look at a scenario where a manager, Kendra, must manage a disengaged employee wearing a Sun Hat and see what elements of the B.E.E.F. Model you can see in action.

When Kendra had been promoted to Director of Culture at the City of Riverside, she was thrilled. Though she didn't know much about arts and culture, she'd shown her strength at managing people in her previous position in Transportation. It was a good promotion and a real challenge because culture had been getting all sorts of attention within the City of Riverside lately.

The federal and regional governments had recently made new funding for major infrastructure projects available. Because the existing policy was that 1% of infrastructure money for any new public construction project was earmarked for public art, the increased budget meant that the RFP (request for proposal) process was suddenly much more attractive. International artists with significantly more experience in major public art works were suddenly outclassing local and regional applications. However, their world-class vision was decidedly more avant-garde than the citizens of sleepy little Riverside were prepared for.

The straw that broke the camel's back was "Hu(man)kind", a 4,000-pound florescent pink reclining figure installed at the cost of half a million dollars. The abstract but anatomically correct form lounged alongside the highway at the city limits, its legs spread lewdly, its private parts facing oncoming traffic. Riverside's conservative newspaper immediately nicknamed the sculpture, "Pervert Gumby" and set about whipping public outrage into a frenzy. The result was the Mayor and three quarters of council were voted out of office and the former head of Culture was given an early retirement package.

The first order of business, Kendra's new boss told her, was the development of a new RFP process for the public art commission. It was to be more transparent to council, more accessible to local artists, and more citizen centric. The City Manager promised the Mayor and Council that this RFP process would be radically different. He told Kendra, "If it's just the 'same old same old' then the mayor's job is on the line, and probably mine too."

Kendra wasn't about to let the project suffer because Alon, the Manager of Public Art, was inexplicably dragging his heels on the revised RFP.

Lights up on Kendra's office at The City of Riverside, a medium-sized city. Alon pokes his head in the door. Kendra directs Alon to the chair opposite her.

KENDRA: Thanks for coming in Alon. I want to review where we are at with the revised RFP process.

ALON: Oh, I'm more or less on target. I think we'll be fine.

KENDRA: I'm looking for something with a lot

more certainty than "I think". Can you give me some specifics?

ALON: It'll be on your desk by the 31st.

KENDRA: That's an issue. It's due before council in three weeks and our General Manager has to review it with the Senior Management Team before that. And I'd like to review the entire proposal before I give it to the GM.

Alon frowns.

ALON: I wasn't aware that both you and the GM wanted to review the proposal before it went to SMT.

KENDRA: I'm not going to give a document to the GM to pass on that I haven't even seen.

ALON: That's not the way we did it with Ruth Anne.

KENDRA: Ruth Anne's not here anymore. Things are changing.

DIANE (*muttering*): They certainly are.

KENDRA: How do you mean that?

Pause.

ALON: I guess I mean it's a big change.

KENDRA: This is a complete overhaul to a
            program that's caused a firestorm
            in the media. I want to be kept in
            the loop.

ALON: I see.

KENDRA: So, let's review where we are at with
            the revised RFP process.

*Alon opens a folder and begins to sort
through its contents.*

ALON: I have to warn you, it's a bit all
            over the place right now. I mean,
            it's on its way, but it's just in
            draft state.

KENDRA: That's fine. Let's just see what
            you've got.

Alon slides a document across the table.

ALON: So, this is the revised application
            form.

KENDRA: I'm not seeing what's different?

ALON: Of course. I keep forgetting how new
            you are to all this. This question
            here is new. And here. Here. And
            here.

Kendra looks Alon in the eye.

KENDRA: So, you've added four new questions?

ALON: Five really. This one has been
           tweaked.

KENDRA: I thought the idea was to simplify
           the application, not make it bigger?

ALON: I thought our goal was to refine
           the application so that we can get
           more detail on each submission, so
           that we don't encounter anymore
           public squabbles?

KENDRA: Our job is to make the process more
           accessible so that a variety of
           artists, including local artists,
           can apply.

ALON: I'm not sure five questions - four
           really - constitutes making it
           substantially bigger.

KENDRA: But it doesn't make it substantially
           smaller does it? I thought you were
           going to slim this section down?

ALON: Yeah… that's not really gonna work…

Pause. Kendra sits back in her chair.

KENDRA: Can you explain why?

ALON: The old system doesn't allow that.

KENDRA: I thought you were re-building the
           form on the new system?

ALON: Oh yes, of course, but I.T. can't

allocate time on this ticket
request to import the old form into
the new system. So, we'll have to
stick with the original form in the
old system.

Kendra raises an eyebrow.

ALON: They can, but not in this quarter.
            So, it can't work within our
            required timeline.

KENDRA: Well, that's a load of crap.

ALON: Yes, I think so too. But I certainly
            don't have the authority to over
            ride I.T.

KENDRA: The General Manager does.

ALON: I'm not the GM.

KENDRA   (*tersely*): That's my job in all this
            Alon. You tell me that I.T. is putting
            up a roadblock, I talk to I.T. If they
            can't or won't prioritize this
            project, then I can call on our G.M.,
            but I can't do any of that if you
            don't tell me.

ALON: OK. That's good to know.

Another pause.

KENDRA: Let's move on to the selection
            process and the role of the Jury
            system in choosing an artwork.

How's the evolution of that going?

ALON: Yes, well, as you suggested, we're increasing public input by adding new positions to the jury for members of the general public.

KENDRA: How many?

ALON: Two.

KENDRA: Out of?

ALON: Twelve. Well, fourteen, once we add these two new voices.

KENDRA: And the other twelve are…?

ALON: Two professors from the Art College and two from the University's Architecture Department. Two curators from the Museum. There's two councillors and two staff from the Culture Department (that's me and my assistant). And, of course, we've always had two external experts, usually from the Metropolitan Museum of Art in New York and another from Boston.

KENDRA: And so, the new addition is these two members of the public?

ALON: Yes.

KENDRA: And that's the extent of the public

engagement process you've developed?

ALON: It'll be a lot of work for the Advisory to bring two lay people up to speed.

KENDRA (*exasperated*): Look, Alon, do I have to spell it out for you? The new Mayor and Council want a new process.

ALON: It's all so political…

KENDRA: Yes, that's why it's called politics. This isn't going to cut it in the new political reality we find ourselves in. You're going to have to completely revamp the public input component.

ALON: Ooooh, that's not going to be easy. I don't know what that would look like.

KENDRA: That's the problem, isn't it Alon? What does a process that includes substantially more input from citizens look like? That's your challenge. Do you think you can do that?

ALON (*resigned*): I'll try.

Alon stands to leave.

KENDRA: Do you remember Star Wars, Alon?

ALON   (*confused*): Star Wars?

KENDRA: Yoda? The little green guy? "There
            is no try. There is only do."

Alon nods. He closes the door behind him.

Taking A Look Backstage

In Act Two, we've presented you with a scenario that is a bit more nuanced and complex than our Viking Helmet. Whereas in Act One, it was pretty clear that our Viking Helmet wearing Veronique was wielding her sword. It's not quite as clear if Alon is on the beach or in the Tiki Bar.

In fact, both are correct. An employee can begin a conversation on the beach happily reading a novel, but when challenged on their behaviour, they can pack up their things in a huff and retire to the Tiki Bar, order a cocktail and contentedly watch the ship crash into the shoals. We saw that happen when Alon said, "Yeah... that's not really gonna work."

It can just as easily happen the other way around. An unmanageable employee can be holding court in the Tiki Lounge with other Sun Hats, but when challenged on their behaviour, they can give the appearance of returning to work only to sullenly slink over to the beach towel when you're not paying attention. We can see that happening with Alon at the end of the scene when he says, "I'll try."

Evaluation

Now that you've had the opportunity to watch a Sun Hat in action, let's analyse what we've observed and how it differs from a Viking Helmet.

1. In your opinion was Alon
- ☐ on the beach?
- ☐ in the Tiki Lounge?

List three behaviours you observed which convinced you of this.

i. _____

ii. _____

iii. _____

2. When we work with employees who are unmanageable, or to phrase it in a more generous way, when we work with employees who have adopted behaviours that are difficult to manage, we often pass judgments. Judgments are often emotional responses masquerading as logical statements. Without thinking too much about it, listen to your gut and list three emotions you observed in yourself that arose when Alon was wearing her Sun Hat.

i. _____

ii. _____

iii. _____

3. If you had the opportunity to coach Kendra on how to approach Alon about her behaviour what is the single most important piece of advice you'd give?

_____

_____

4. By the end of the dialogue how likely do you think Alon is to change?

1	2	3	4	5	6	7	8	9	10
Not Likely								Very Likely	

There may have even been some elements of Alon's behaviour that reminded you of someone wearing a Viking Helmet, particularly when Alon was being passive aggressive. You're not wrong. Just as an individual may move from the beach to the Tiki Bar, they may remove their Sun Hat and temporarily put on a Viking Helmet. Shortly thereafter, they may even toss their helmet into the dust in disgust, pull their Sun Hat over their ears and stomp off to the beach to pout. If that level of volatility disheartens you, then welcome to the real world. The metaphor of the four hats isn't intended to provide simple rigid categories into which complex dynamic human behaviour can be permanently classified.

When tackling complex behaviour issues, common wisdom suggests stacking your concerns, prioritizing the most important issue, and working your way down the list. We think that the result is likely to overwhelm and create disengagement. It's common for anyone to shut down when under threat. It's a primitive fight or flight response that is marked by physical changes. Adrenaline floods the blood stream and activates the body's sympathetic nervous system. Heart rate increases to prepare the individual to run if possible. Breathing and blood pressure increases to prepare you to fight if necessary. Pupils dilate and their focus narrows, so they are not distracted by anything other than the immediate threat before them. In the midst of all this, you then expect your employee to absorb a laundry list of behaviour you want them to change.

Successful leaders have discovered that the key to clear communication is to have one key message and only one key message. Ken spent many years providing presentation

coaching to executives and this advice was always central. Invariably, leaders would push back and lament that they had three or four or five key messages to communicate. "No, you don't," Ken would insist. "You have one key message, with five supporting bullet points." It's easy to confuse supporting bullet points with key messages because, usually, the supporting bullet points come to mind first.

We recommend that you avoid thinking of behaviours in isolation. Instead, think of your employee as an iceberg. The bit of the iceberg that we see, the behaviour, is only approximately 10% of the total mass. The majority lies under the water's surface. Like icebergs, behaviours are outward manifestations of something that is going on underneath the surface. And like an iceberg, the submerged portion spreads out in all directions, making approach even more dangerous. Therefore, we encourage you to find out what belief underlies the behaviour.

Kendra faces just this dilemma. There are many important things she wants to say about Alon's behaviour. In Take One, she tries to tackle them all in a single conversation. As a result, she lacks focus and Alon has trouble following what is being said. When it becomes too difficult, she just gives up. In essence, by trying to say many things, Kendra ends up saying nothing.

Try the exercise on the following page to figure out what is motivating your employee's unmanageable behaviour. We encourage you to apply it to a real life individual you work with who is wearing a Sun Hat. If you haven't got an individual in your organization wearing a Sun Hat, lucky you! Feel free to use Alon as your example.

Identifying The Root Of Behaviour

1. Think about someone exhibiting Sun Hat behaviour in your organization.
List as many of the behaviours you have observed as you can.

_____   _____

_____   _____

_____   _____

_____   _____

_____   _____

_____   _____

2. Rewrite the list, grouping behaviours into as few categories as possible. Try to
group like behaviours together. When you're done, try to give each category a title
that we'll call a "master behaviour".

Master behaviour   Master behaviour

_____   _____

_____   _____

_____   _____

Master behaviour   Master behaviour

_____   _____

_____   _____

_____   _____

3. If your employee were to change only ONE of the Master Behaviours you've identified above, which would transform your working relationship most?

_____

_____

_____

_____

We feel the last question is the most fruitful, because it can lead to the ONE BIG ISSUE. That's what holds the greatest promise of long-lasting impact.

It's likely that you have many immediate priorities and you want to deal with the easier issues rather than the ONE BIG ISSUE. You may even be in a crisis. At these times, it's natural to focus on immediate tasks. Unfortunately, in today's business environment, there *never* seems to be a time when things calm down. Even once things have calmed down, it's all too easy to fool ourselves into thinking that the ONE BIG ISSUE, isn't that big a deal after all or that our Sun Hat will take care of themselves.

It is our belief that, as a leader, you and your organization would benefit most from setting aside short-term goals such as simply getting the job done. Instead, use the opportunity to address the ONE BIG ISSUE that can pay benefits in the short, medium *and* long term.

ACT TWO, SCENE TWO

Kendra stared at the clock and imagined what it would be like to fire Alon. She ran the numbers in her head and realized that the severance package, plus the cost of searching for and training his replacement, would be roughly equal to the equivalent of 6, maybe 9 months' salary. Even still, she wondered if it was worth the price to be rid of Alon.

Kendra shook her head. Those kinds of thoughts weren't helpful. No one knew the ins and outs of the public art program like Alon. He was trusted by all the individuals involved, both on the Public Art Committee and within the art community who composed the jury for each competition. He had a great deal of social capital that could be used to leverage change. If only Alon himself could overcome his limiting behaviours.

Kendra looked at the list of behaviours she'd drawn up and tried to group them together. Alon was resistant to change. He was married to the old program. He dismissed most suggestions that Kendra offered. However, Kendra knew she had to get deeper than that.

When Kendra reflected on the past several weeks, she recalled several occasions when Alon spoke disparagingly of public input. He considered the backlash about the artwork that the committee had commissioned and installed to be inconsequential. Kendra recorded those behaviours and wrote "engagement" at the head of that column.

Whenever Kendra would explain what the Mayor and Council wanted to see in terms of public consultation, Alon

would nod. But there seemed to be little or no sense of urgency. Kendra wrote "stakes" at the head of that column.

Alon was recalcitrant. He was inconsistent. He said one thing and did another. He agreed to a course of action and then abruptly reversed course. That seemed to be a bundle that belonged together. Kendra rewrote those items into a single column and labelled it "accountability".

Kendra glanced at the clock on the wall. Two minutes until the meeting began. Now she needed to determine which of these so-called "master behaviours" was the most urgent. Alon's dismissal of the value of engagement was distressing but that was a subset of the greater topic that had been labelled "stakes." Kendra zeroed in on the column labelled "accountability." She circled it. That was it. That was where she needed to start.

Kendra recalled the workshop she had taken on effective, challenging conversations, and wished she had the worksheet that outlined the B.E.E.F. Model close at hand. The facilitators had given her a wallet-sized card that had the four steps outlined on it. She dug through her purse and found it mixed in with some receipts. She set it on the corner of her desk where she could glance at it if needed.

At that moment the door opened.

Lights Up. Alon pokes his head in door.

KENDRA: Hi Alon, thanks for coming.

ALON: Of course.

Alon sits.

KENDRA: I want to review this RFP process.
            In particular, I want to begin by
            focusing on the way we've been
            communicating around expectations
            and deliverables. Or, I guess, not
            communicating.

ALON: Uh-huh... You feel I haven't been
            communicating?

KENDRA: What I've been noticing is that when
            we meet and talk through next
            steps we seem to be on the same
            page, but when you return with a
            revised plan, very little has
            changed.

Alon sits back, a little defensively.

ALON: I think we've made great strides,
            all things considered.

KENDRA: Let me give you an example of what
            I mean. One of the biggest elements
            that the new Council wants to see
            implemented is substantially more
            public input. In the months since, I
            haven't seen a concrete proposal

for what that could look like.

ALON: We've talked through a bunch of options.

KENDRA: We've talked about a lot of options, but we haven't landed on one.

ALON: We added two new positions for members of the public to the Public Art Jury. That's a pretty big step.

KENDRA: It's only two people, added to a jury of fourteen. Which ultimately means that public input is drowned out by expert opinion. What the Mayor and Council are expecting is a series of town hall meetings in the neighbourhoods where the artwork will be placed. They are expecting online engagement tools. A media strategy. An opportunity for real substantial input from the public. Do you remember we talked about that?

ALON: Yes, I remember the discussion. But we didn't land on anything concrete.

KENDRA: This is an example of what I mean. We discuss a variety of potential options, but most of them fall off the table and are never heard from again.

ALON: You left it up to me to weigh the options.

KENDRA: I left it up to you to flesh out the options and return with two or three draft proposals. Perhaps going forward we need to be a little clearer on what the expected next steps are because the effect that it's having is an erosion of trust.

ALON: You're saying you don't trust me now?

KENDRA: I'm saying I don't trust that we're on the same page. As a result, I don't trust that we have the same understanding of the expectations and deliverables. An even bigger one is that I don't trust that we're going to hit our deadline.

ALON: Well, the application form is in the folder I gave you. It just needs your approval.

Alon slides a document across the table to Kendra. Kendra slides it to one side.

KENDRA: I'd like to stay on the topic of accountability. Let's set the application form to one side for now.

ALON: Well, it's a pretty big part of the RFP.

KENDRA: To my mind, the engagement plan is a bigger part of the redesign.

ALON: Well, I'm not really prepared to dive into that right now.

KENDRA: Exactly Alon. I think that's the problem that we're facing. We've put off discussing the engagement plan and the effect is, that we're starting to run out of runway.

ALON: Our current process has developed organically over nearly a decade, and it has worked pretty well over most of that time.

KENDRA: The facts say otherwise. Things were fine when this was a smaller program but now that the program is substantially bigger, there's been a series of scandals.

ALON: But this shouldn't be about politics, this should be about art. There are always furores when it comes to public art. They blow over.

KENDRA: This is not going to blow over.

ALON: Look at the Book of Man.

KENDRA: The what?

ALON: Oh, sorry, sometimes I forget how young you are.

Kendra takes a sharp intake of breath, but she bites her tongue and says nothing. Alon doesn't notice and continues.

ALON: When those statues were first installed in the 1960s people were appalled that, aside from the books, the figures were naked. Now it's so beloved by the public that it's the logo for the Public Library. People point to it and say, "Why can't we have more of that?"

KENDRA: That's the kind of feedback that we have to respond to.

ALON: I'm saying that's just the kind of feedback we can't respond to. As a city, as a society, we grow into public art. And it's a process that happens not over weeks or months, but over decades. That's precisely why we can't let public opinion contaminate the decision-making process.

KENDRA: I think we've just found the core of the problem Alon. We have to stop thinking of public input as a "contamination" of the process. It's called "public art" not "city art". We have to start viewing the input of the public as the process.

ALON: That's… that's…

KENDRA: A big change. I know. When council asks for a substantial redesign of our process, that means they want a big change.

Pause. Kendra allows this information to sink in. Alon fiddles with his notebook.

ALON: I don't really know where to start. This is not something we're used to doing with this program.

KENDRA: Transportation does large-scale engagements of this sort all the time. I can introduce you to some of their people. Would that be a place to start?

ALON: That seems like a good idea.

Kendra makes a note in her book.

KENDRA: I'll do that today.

ALON: In the meantime, let's talk about this application form.

Alon reaches for the document and positions it back in front of Kendra.

Evaluation

Now that you've had the opportunity to watch the B.E.E.F. Model in action a second time, let's analyze what we've observed.

1. Re-read Scene Two looking just at Kendra's lines. Try to identify at which points Kendra is:

- Speaking about Alon's BEHAVIOUR
- Providing EXAMPLES of his behaviour
- Identifying the EFFECTS of his behaviour
- Requesting different behaviour in the FUTURE

2. Now re-read the same dialogue, but this time looking just at Alon's lines

- Draw a hat beside those moments where Alon puts on his Sun Hat.
- Observe the strategies Kendra employs to defuse the behaviour.

3. On a scale of 1 to 10 how likely do you think Alon is to remove his Sun Hat and change his behaviour in the future?

1	2	3	4	5	6	7	8	9	10
Not likely								Very likely	

Taking A Second Look Backstage

In preparing for the conversation before Scene Two, Kendra made a wise decision by being selective about which behaviours she wanted to tackle. As a result, Kendra was better able to focus the conversation than she was in Scene One.

It still wasn't easy. Alon was immediately on the defensive. Right away he said, "I think we've made great strides." Alon even pointed to the new positions he'd created as proof of the work he has accomplished. It's worth noting that Alon wasn't lying when he said this. He really did think that they'd made great strides. He really did think that adding two people to a jury was sufficient public input. It took Kendra to point out that it's not.

Kendra exhibited skill in keeping Alon on track by steering the conversation back to her key point, accountability. This is where determining what key message you want to challenge your employee on pays off. It's difficult to return to your main point when you don't have one. Kendra had not settled on a key message prior to Scene One, and her inability to control the conversation reflected that. In Scene Two, when she felt that conversation was moving off topic, Kendra had a clear statement she could continually return to.

It also helped Kendra discipline and regulate herself so that she was undeterred by passive aggressive behaviours. Kendra was able to refocus her attention instead of reacting or being distracted when Alon uttered the veiled insult, "Sometimes I forget how young you are." This enabled her to listen and hear Alon's more salient point about the Book of Man statue.

By persisting and remaining focused on her key message, Kendra finally uncovered the root of the problem: Alon doesn't trust or want public input. Which ultimately is Alon's shorthand for, "I don't want to change." After a moment's silence, Alon confessed that he doesn't really know where to start because, "This is not something we're used to doing with this program." Kendra was able to offer a concrete proposal for how to move forward and offered to connect Alon with some resources in another department.

Flip back to the evaluation that you conducted at the end of Scene Two, when you scanned the scene for elements of the B.E.E.F. Model. Did you notice something was missing? Kendra neglected to explicitly outline future steps that she wanted Alon to take to correct the problem behaviour. Instead, Kendra defaulted to discussing next steps she wanted Alon to take with regards to the project.

As we'll see, this is a critical omission that is by no means uncommon, but will come back to bite Kendra. It's easy for leaders, overcome with relief at the end of a challenging conversation, to allow themselves to revert to practical solutions when the emotionally hard work appears to be over. However, this is an illusion, the work is not done until it is done.

As with so many things in life, there are consequences to not following through on this last step and saying what's needed. Just as there are consequences to how you say it.

Evaluating Your Own Sun Hat

In Act One, we asked you to consider occasions when you, as a leader, were wearing a Viking Helmet of your own. Now it's time to once again turn the spotlight on yourself and look for occasions when you may have been abdicating your responsibilities as a leader.

1. Has there ever been an occasion when you have worn a Sun Hat, even if it was only temporary?

_____

_____

_____

2. Were you wearing your Sun Hat on the beach or in the Tiki Bar? What behaviours did you demonstrate?

_____

_____

_____

3. If you had the opportunity to go back in time and coach your old boss on how to call you out on your behaviour, what is the one piece of advice you'd give her/him?

_____

_____

_____

Remember a person wearing a Sun Hat is used to problems working themselves out, usually because someone else solves the problem for them. Whenever you utter phrases like, "I'm sure it'll work out" or "Let's see how it goes" you know you're wearing a Sun Hat.

PUT YOUR LANGUAGE UNDER THE MICROSCOPE

In a moment we're going to look at Scene Three. Before we do, let's take a moment to look through a microscope at the building blocks of conversation: the language. When leading a challenging conversation with your employees, it's important to be intentional about the words and phrases you use.

You want to be *challenging* your employees, not *criticizing* them. We've said several times and in different ways, that your challenging conversation needs to focus on the problem and not on the *person*. That distinction is conveyed, at the most granular level, in the language you use. You can believe you are offering a challenging conversation all you want, but if the language you are using consists of phrases such as, "I think you are a problem around here" (or worse, "I need to F**xxx**ing talk to you") then you are criticising, not challenging.

Here are some general principles to guide the language you're using. We've aligned each principle with an element of the B.E.E.F. Model.

> **Stick to the *facts*, and avoid *judgement*.** You need to maintain your focus on what *actually* happened, not on what you *think* happened. It's all too easy to slip phrases such as "I think" or "I feel" or "in my opinion", into the conversation. If a leader says, "I think you're avoiding the work assigned to you", then a

Sun Hat could reasonably reply, "I don't think so". Your employee either did the work to your satisfaction or she did not. He either crossed the line with his behaviour, or he did not. You do no one any favours by softening your language and leaving room for doubt or argument later. This is why, in the B.E.E.F. Model, we encourage you to focus on the behaviour, because it's much easier to be objective and stick to the facts.

Be *specific*, and not *general*. You cannot effectively describe behaviour without providing specific examples. Saying, "Sometimes you come in late" leaves room to think, "That's fine, because it means I'm mostly punctual". This is why in the B.E.E.F. Model, we insist you provide specific examples. You can also be specific in all elements of the conversation by being precise in your description of the behaviour you've observed, explicit with the effects you've observed on others, and unambiguous about the future behaviour you want to see.

Reinforce *relationship* rather than create *division*. Any conversation can be viewed as an effort to draw closer to someone or push them further away. You'll need to work with this individual in the future, so it's not beneficial to create a rift that makes it less likely for them to trust you, come to you with problems, or confide in you when they're troubled. As you may recall, it's not just about you. The B.E.E.F. Model instructs you to speak to the effects their behaviour has had on their co-workers, so you also need to use language that bolsters the working relationship between your employees, rather than creates discord between them.

Change their behaviour, don't *blame* the person. If the only reason you are having the conversation is because your boss kicked you and you're looking for the next person down the line to give a kick to, then you're not being a leader. The final step of the B.E.E.F. Model, the emphasis on the future behaviour you wish to see, epitomizes this advice but it's applicable at all stages. The language you use should, at all costs, focus on the change you want to see, so they can do their job more effectively.

This focus on language does not imply that you can't express displeasure or strong emotion. In fact, following these guidelines frees you up to speak directly to poor performance and give voice to how you feel about it, within the safety of a structured conversation.

Russell recalls overhearing a strongly worded conversation when he worked for the HM Customs and Excise in London between a supervising officer in the local investigation team and two of his junior officers who had botched a surveillance operation. Through the closed door Russell, and everyone else on the floor, could clearly hear the supervisor using foul language at extreme volumes. Yet, they were not themselves vile people and, despite his displeasure and their poor performance, at no point did the supervisor treat them with disrespect. Later, when the brass demanded he give up the names of his officers for reprimand, the supervisor refused. He stated that as the supervisor, he was the one who was responsible for the outcome of the investigation.

In Scene Three, let's watch while Kendra deals with the consequences of not being clear with future steps at the conclusion of Scene Two. See if you can observe the extent to which she is or is not being intentional with her language and if she is able to do so without pulling any punches.

ACT TWO, SCENE THREE

Lights up. Alon closes the door behind him and takes a seat in front of Kendra.

KENDRA: Thanks for coming in Alon. I had a chance to review what you've sent me.

ALON: Yes, we've really been making progress, haven't we?

KENDRA: There's no mention in here of the engagement plan.

ALON: Yes, well, I'm still working on that.

KENDRA: And have you got anything to show me?

ALON: It's all still a bit... amorphous.

KENDRA: Amorphous?

ALON: Almost… insubstantial.

Kendra lets the uncomfortable silence hang in the air for a moment.

KENDRA: Why don't you tell me what you've been doing so far.

ALON: I met with the engagement specialists from Transportation and they left me with some good ideas. But implementing them is going to take a significant part of the budget.

KENDRA: And that's your concern?

ALON: It's been the City's policy to keep as much of the funds going to the artists as possible. The cost of all this public engagement will drive those costs up further, meaning there's less funding for the actual art.

KENDRA: We have to accept that it's the cost of getting public buy-in for the program.

ALON: That's too high a price to pay. We'd be taking that money directly out of the hands of artists. And compromising the quality of the art.

KENDRA: Not engaging in some form of public consultation is not an option.

ALON: We are engaging the public already. How much more do they want?

KENDRA: So here we see the behaviour again that we talked about last time.

ALON: How so?

KENDRA: We agreed on a course of action, that you'd check in with transportation and get some advice and return with a public consultation model.

ALON: I have done that. You just don't like the conclusions I've come up with.

KENDRA: That's because your conclusion is to do nothing. I ask you to move forward and instead you stay put. The effect is a) an erosion of trust and b) we're running out of time.

ALON: I just... I can't see a way forward that preserves the program. And I can't see how we're going to sell it to the Public Art Committee that supervises the jury process.

KENDRA: Let me be a little provocative here. It's the City's funding. Isn't getting approval from a committee on how the City consults with the public a little like the tail wagging the dog?

ALON: We rely on their expert opinion to avoid cost overruns on manufacturing and installation costs. They're essentially volunteering their time. They're not going to do that if they can't support the outcome.

KENDRA: That makes sense. But again let me be a little provocative. How much of your current resistance is because you're afraid of what your peers on the committee and in the art world will think of these changes?

Silence.

It's OK for that to be a factor. We're human.

ALON: I suppose it is a factor.

KENDRA: Of course. In fact, it would be odd if personal relationships weren't a factor. Now here's the next obvious question. Do you feel that you're too close to this project? Sometimes, when we've been with a program for so long, we fall in love with the way it was, and we can't see through to the way it needs to be.

ALON: Do you want me off this project?

KENDRA: No. I truly believe that with your depth of experience and understanding, you're the one to see it through to a new phase.

ALON: It's just so hard …

KENDRA: It is. Especially because you've invested in its success for 10 years. Look at it this way; you've built an appetite amongst the public. They now see art as an important part of their city, and they want to be involved. The consequences of denying them a place in the discussion is that we might lose the program altogether.

Another pause. Alon takes a deep breath and looks Kendra in the eye.

ALON: Maybe we can use the Hayes Bridge as a model.

KENDRA: How so?

ALON: I'm sorry, I keep forgetting how young you are. The City tore down the Hayes Bridge seven years ago.

KENDRA: I'm not that much younger than you. Plus I grew up in that neighbourhood. I remember the bridge.

ALON: I'm sorry. I didn't mean to be

disrespectful. To be honest, I envy your vitality. Sometimes I feel I've been at this too long, like you said.

KENDRA: Tell me about the Hayes Bridge.

ALON: It's not so much the bridge that's important. It's what the community did after the bridge was torn down. The original bridge had been named after Louise Hayes, and it was the only public infrastructure named after a woman. So, the community insisted when we sent out the tender that the artist needed to be willing to consult with residents.

KENDRA: And how did that turn out?

ALON: Very successfully. The jury selected an artist from Capital City but someone who had lived in Riverside for a decade, so she knew the community firsthand. The community was very pleased with the result. And the art itself was very high calibre.

KENDRA: So, what elements from that Hayes Bridge project can we take and apply to this?

ALON: Well… a lot of what we did on that project is similar to what the engagement team at Transportation has been recommending.

KENDRA: So, can that success story serve as
            a model going forward?

ALON: I think it can, yes.

KENDRA: Will using the Hayes Bridge Project
            as a model help with your
            conversations with the committee
            going forward?

ALON: Good point. They'll feel more
            comfortable if I can point to a past
            success.

Alon pauses for a moment and then laughs.

            Plus, it always helps when they
            think it's their idea.

KENDRA   (*laughs*): I can say the same thing
            about council. But in all
            seriousness, we can position this as
            a "made in Riverside" solution. Do
            you think this is starting to feel
            like a way forward?

ALON: I think so, yes.

KENDRA: Me too. Are you willing to draft a
            public engagement strategy that
            utilizes what you've learned from
            the Engagement Specialists at
            Transportation and frame it in the
            context of the success of the
            Bridge project?

ALON: I think so, yes.

KENDRA: If we are going to make this
           deadline then it's vital that you
           hold yourself accountable to this
           commitment Alon. Are you up for
           that?

ALON: Yes. We really need to do what's best
           for the program in the long run.

*Kendra flips over the paper and begins to
write on the back.*

KENDRA: Let me outline what I think the
           document we have to present to
           council next week needs to look
           like.

Evaluation

Now that you've had the opportunity to watch the B.E.E.F. Model in action a third time, let's analyze what we've observed.

1. What were the consequences of Kendra's failure in Act Two, Scene Two to explicitly outline future steps that she wanted Alon to take to correct the problem behaviour, which you observed in Act Two, Scene Three?

_____

_____

_____

2. Now that Kendra has had to have this discussion again, on a scale of 1 to 10 how likely do you think Alon is to remove his Sun Hat and change his behaviour in the future?

1	2	3	4	5	6	7	8	9	10
Not Likely								Very Likely	

3. If you rated Alon as likely to change or somewhat likely to change, what do you view as the turning point in the conversation? Can you circle that portion of dialogue?

4. Did you observe Kendra:

☐ Challenging not criticizing.
☐ Focusing on the problem and not on the person.
☐ Sticking to the facts, and avoiding judgement.
☐ Being specific, and not general.
☐ Reinforcing relationship rather than creating division.
☐ Focus on changing the behaviour vs blaming the person.

Who's Your Boss?

At the end of Scene Three, Kendra succeeds in doing what she failed to do at the conclusion of Scene Two: provide Alon with a clear set of future actions she wants him to take. When we skip that step, we leave the next steps open to interpretation. Some individuals, whenever allowed an option, will easily slip on their Sun Hat and retire to the beach where it's comfortable.

This is precisely what Alon did. He began Scene Three thinking that he had, in all honesty, done what was asked of him. *Engagement Plan? Oh, yeah, that. It runs counter to what I was told ten years ago about keeping administrative overhead low. Investigation complete. My work here is done. Back to the beach.*

Alon has his heart in the right place. He wants to keep money in the hands of artists and keep administrative costs low. In this regard, he's following orders. Old orders, ones he prefers. Alon is also keeping the standards high and preserving the quality of the art. Even if Kendra, the council and the citizens disagree with him, they'll learn in time. Perhaps you have employees who refuse to compromise on quality in the face of direct orders.

These are valuable priorities, but they are not the current priorities of his employer, The City of Riverside. Alon's position at the outset of Scene Three, is an example of what can happen when an employee is confused about who exactly, is their boss. Alon thinks he is in service to the arts community, and to some extent to the greater good of the community.

But his boss really is The City of Riverside[8] and that boss has a set of priorities that are at odds with Alon's principles. Depending on your view of the role of public art in society, you may feel that Alon occupies the moral high ground. Perhaps public art should court controversy and push the bounds of taste. Given the long term horizons, maybe it is a good idea for public art to stand aloof from the pendulum of public opinion. There is a sound economic argument that attracting artists of international renown, puts Riverside on the map and drives tourism. However, these are not Alon's arguments to make. If he wants to make them, he should write a letter to his councillor as a private citizen, start a Facebook campaign or run for office himself.

Uncovering an employee who is more loyal to the program than to their employer, is common in public administration and the social service sector. Given the stereotype of lazy public sector bureaucrats, this may come as a surprise, but it shouldn't. Pay in the social services is typically lower than in the corporate sphere, opportunities for advancement are comparatively rare, and the sector is regularly accused of overspending. The public sector regularly lays off employees whenever there is a change in government. Public servants are regularly called on the carpet by media and even their neighbours sometimes view them as lazy obstructionists. Who in their right mind would want to work in an environment where their every move is inspected, judged and publicly ridiculed?

The answer is, those who are driven by passion. Social service sector workers are typically motivated by an intense de-

[8] If we want to get really pedantic, The Mayor and Council have only one employee, the City Manager who is then responsible to hire everyone else, so they can carry out the vision of the Council. This is a mirror of a corporate hierarchy, in which the shareholders of a private corporation have only one employee in the person of the CEO. This division of power safeguards civic employees from having to respond to rogue council members, just as it does in the corporate world.

sire to make the lives of the disadvantaged better or to correct a social ill. Public sector employees are equally passionate about making their city a better place. Individuals can become more loyal to a program that they see as fulfilling this altruistic function than they are to their employers whom they may view as being driven by less noble motives. It's as if these individuals are confused as to who is their boss, the program or The City, the client or the charity, the society or the corporation.

If you are in private business, you don't have to look far to find employees with misplaced passion who are loyal to a program rather than the corporation. Think about points of resistance you may have encountered over the years from employees who become enamoured with a pet project or innovative solution and are frustrated or angry when a project gets shelved. That's when we see employees check out, don their Sun Hat and head to the beach.

It's at this point that many individuals would run out of patience and lose their temper. In such a situation, you may feel that you've had to repeat yourself too many times, that your Sun Hat isn't getting the message, and that their behaviour is never going to change. You may feel like you're talking to a recalcitrant child or a wilful teenager. You may feel that you're stuck in a recurring time loop like Bill Murray in the film *Groundhog Day*. It's at this point that many leaders would be tempted to throw up their hands and fire an employee like Alon, or at the very least, have him transferred to someone else's department, so they can become someone else's problem.

Not Kendra. In Scene Three, she exercised a heroic level of patience.

As a leader, you have to accept that sometimes it takes multiple attempts for the message to get through. Anyone who has ever tried to quit smoking can recognize that changing behaviours is hard, and it takes time. If it was easy, everyone would do it. Kendra finally gets to the heart of Alon's resistance when she uncovers his concern for his relationships with the committee, relationships he has spent nearly a decade building. Kendra has a surprising amount of empathy for Alon at this moment.

This reveals something vital to a challenging conversation. It's only when Kendra and Alon have identified the root of the problem that they are finally able to brainstorm a solution and a future action. It's at this precise moment that Alon finally exchanges his Sun Hat for a Hard Hat. Having accepted that his current behaviour is serving no one (least of all the program he values), Alon is finally able to move forward. It is now that Kendra shifts from a challenging conversation to a coaching conversation. Interestingly, it's not Kendra who comes up with the solution, it's Alon. Kendra simply fleshes out the idea by asking pointed questions at key moments.

By the end of Scene Three, Kendra has explicitly stated what future action she expects and what shape she wants it to take. In the last lines of the scene, Kendra is actually drafting the outline for Alon for the sake of further clarity. Some of you may feel that Kendra's decision to outline the proposal for Alon is a step too far, and that now Kendra is doing

Alon's work for him. It's true that sometimes, a Sun Hat will feign ignorance of what's expected, in the hopes that someone will pick up the slack and just do it for them. However, that's not what seems to be happening here. It seems that Alon is genuinely ready to move forward but that he needs guidance.

This is the essence of someone wearing a Hard Hat. They want to move towards a solution, but they need help. They're looking to you to provide them with a blueprint. Kendra would have been remiss if she *hadn't* provided that blueprint to Alon when the opportunity presented itself. In fact, had Alon not received the coaching he needed at that moment, the odds are high that he would slip his Sun Hat back on.

In Acts 3 and 4, we will look at two coaching conversations in action. We will observe how coaching can help a Hard Hat get clear on what they need to do next. We'll see how it can help guide a Graduate Cap away from failure and towards success. But first we will take a deep dive into one of several simple coaching models that can be used to shape a conversation.

It's time for an intermission.

SUMMARY

The individual wearing a Sun Hat is as common in a contemporary workplace as those wearing a Viking Helmet, but they are not quite as negative as a Viking Helmet. They're also a lot harder to catch in the act because they disguise or justify their actions.

Employees wearing a Sun Hat can be grouped into two broad categories:

- The Sun Hat on The Beach is so disengaged, they might as well be reading a trashy novel on the beach.
- The Sun Hat in The TikiBar, retires to the sidelines where they watch in relative comfort while others do the work.

These are not strict categories. An individual may be wearing a Sun Hat and complaining in the Tiki Bar one moment, only to put on a Viking Helmet and take up their shield the next, and later retire to the beach.

You want to be challenging your employees, not criticizing them, by focusing on the problem and not on the person. That distinction is conveyed, at the most granular level, in the language you use.

Avoid overwhelming a Sun Hat with a laundry list of complaints, or you risk further disengaging them. If you try to say too much, you end up saying nothing memorable. Be selective about problem behaviours you want to tackle. Distill what you want to say to a key message and continue to return to it over the course of the conversation.

Not every Sun Hat fits the stereotype of a lazy employee. Sometimes, it may be that they have their priorities misplaced. For instance, an employee may be more devoted to a program or to a customer base. It's important to find out what's motivating their disengagement.

Once a Sun Hat has accepted their behaviour needs to change, then they have effectively put on a hard hat. Then they can be coached.

INTERMISSION

Leading In The Second Half Using The C.O.A.C.H. Model

During the intermission, we'll explore a coaching model that can help you get the highest performance from those team members wearing Hard Hats and Graduate Caps. Its cleverly called C.O.A.C.H. to make it easy to remember. We will examine why questions are more important in coaching than answers. We'll take a deep dive into each phase of the C.O.A.C.H. Model and look at sample questions that can be used in each phase to lead your Hard Hats and Graduate Caps to their own solutions.

BEHIND THE BENCH, NOT ON IT

As a leader, it's your role to help your team achieve their best. It's not your job to take on their responsibilities or to micro-manage them. In fact, doing so is often counter-productive because it shuts your employees down and leads them to think they can't do it correctly for themselves. Worse, it leads you into a bottleneck, leaving you responsible for an increasing number of decisions and actions.

When we discussed the Four Hats earlier, we noted that the Sun Hat and the Viking Helmet can't really be coached because it's hard to coach someone who refuses to admit there's a problem. By this point, you've had that challenging conversation and convinced them to exchange their hats for a Hard Hat or a Graduate Cap. Now you can switch tracks and focus on being a coach.

One of the greatest challenges facing a leader is the shift between thinking of yourself as the star player who takes centre-field to thinking of yourself as the coach who stands behind a bench filled with high-performance athletes. It would be ridiculous to see a hockey coach go onto the ice and play the puck for the players in the middle of a game, or to see a football coach go onto the field and show the defence how to block the tackles, or for a basketball coach to run onto the court and move players to a new position. In fact, a team would be heavily penalized and a coach would be fired on the spot!

In fact, the coach is the last person you want making those small decisions. The coach's job is just the opposite; their role is to train the team so that they can make the best decisions possible while they are in the heat of the moment. By doing this, you'll help them make better decisions, solve problems that are holding them back, learn new skills, and otherwise progress their careers. The more effective the coach is at coaching, the less he or she has to do at the micro level, and the more time the coach can spend on strategy and performance-related issues.

Some people are fortunate enough to get formal training in coaching and sometimes their company invests heavily in training its managers. However, many individuals work at companies that either can't afford such training or don't see the value in it. In working with numerous organizations in the public, private and non-profit sectors, Russell has found that managers are usually promoted into their positions because they have the requisite technical experience, not because they've proven themselves adept at bringing out the best in their co-workers. As far as the hiring process is concerned, if these individuals have well-developed people skills, then it's a bonus rather than a requirement.

It doesn't necessarily follow that if we know the equipment or processes inside and out, that we intuitively know how to coach individuals who are struggling so they can transform into high performers. It seems common sense when you see it in writing but in practice, too many managers are forced to develop this important skill through trial and error or by following their instincts.

If you've been appointed a leader, then your instincts are likely very good. It might help you enhance those instincts if you can use them within a simple, easy to remember but powerful and effective framework, like the C.O.A.C.H. Model.

There are a number of common coaching models used and they all have a number of easy to remember acronyms. As you've already seen, we're big on acronyms in our workshops and take-home materials (B.E.E.F. anyone?). We find it makes ideas and frameworks sticky, so that you can remember them when your unmanageable employee or team member is sitting in front of you and the pressure is on. Other coaching models on the market have value. However, as you'll see when we dig into the model we offer, C.O.A.C.H. places special emphasis on accountability.

Let's clear up a few questions about questions first.

QUESTIONS VS. ANSWERS

Having written over 25 plays and sat through innumerable new play workshops, Ken has come to the conclusion that, "There are three basic human needs. The need to eat, the need to sleep and the need to rewrite my play for me."

In new play development workshops, it's traditional to hire actors to read the script out loud so the playwright, director and designers can hear the rhythm of the dialogue, feel the pace of the individual scenes and experience the shape of the overall play. When the reading is over, it's common for everyone in the room to offer their feedback, comments and suggestions. According to Ken, feedback sometimes goes something like this:

ACTOR 1:   I don't understand why my character says this.

KEN: It's because he's lying.

ACTOR 1:   I wouldn't say it that way.

KEN: Maybe you wouldn't, but you're not the character.

ACTOR 1:   I'd say it this way.

Insert suggested rewrite here.

KEN: Phrasing it that way means your character comes up with the idea, instead of the wife. It makes your character the active agent.

ACTOR 1:   It seems more natural for me to motivate the line when it's written that way.

KEN: But this scene's not about your character.

ACTOR 2:   This is just a crazy idea but hear me out.

Insert wacky idea that contradicts the research Ken has already done.

Later in the process, feedback to a play is extremely valuable. However, in these early stages, it can actually be detrimental. Ed Catmull, the President and CEO of Pixar Inc., the creative studio behind such monster hits as Toy Story, coined the phrase "Ugly Babies".

> "Early on, all our movies suck. That's a blunt assessment I know, but I chose that phrasing because saying it in a softer way, fails to convey how bad the first versions [of Pixar films] really are. I'm not trying to be modest or self-effacing. Pixar films are not good at first... it's a baby. It's like the fetus of a movie star; we all start out ugly. Every one of Pixar's stories starts out that way. A new thing is hard to define; it's not attractive, and it requires protection[9]."

Ken is proud to say that he follows in Pixar's footsteps and also writes ugly babies in the form of really crappy first drafts. (Maybe, Russell proposes slyly, this is why everyone wants to rewrite them). Mind you, later in the process, Ken's plays tend to please critics, achieve sold-out audiences and get produced across Canada. Before they reach that point his plays are ugly, ugly babies, that not even a mother could love. No matter how ugly they are, Ken is still possessive of them and he bristles when someone tries to rewrite them for him.

Ken confesses shamefacedly that, "It's completely different for me when I'm on the other side of the table, sitting in the director's chair. Then I feel that I can see with great clarity the structural problems that make someone else's ugly baby

[9] The book *Creativity, Inc.: Overcoming the Unseen Forces That Stand in the Way of Inspiration* was co-written by Ed Catmull with journalist Amy Wallace. She never seems to get credited when the book is quoted, so let's make sure Amy Wallace gets acknowledged here.

so disagreeable, and I can't help myself from making suggestions. Because, there are three basic human needs. The need to eat, the need to sleep and the need to rewrite someone else's play." Ken is not especially hypocritical by nature, he's just human. Perhaps you are the same. You might get defensive when your boss is overly critical of your suggestions, but you don't hesitate to be just as harsh with your team members.

There are leaders who recognize this tendency and develop structures that make it easy for everyone to coach appropriately. Theatre Director Bob White is one of them.

Bob has made an indelible impact on the way new plays are written and developed in Canada. After working across Canada, Bob moved to Calgary to take the helm of the renowned playRites Festival of New Canadian Plays and later became Artistic Director of Alberta Theatre Projects. Bob has since taken a position as Director of New Play Development at the Stratford Shakespeare Festival, one of North America's largest and most respected arts institutions.

Bob loves questions so much that he forbids answers. If anyone feels the urge to offer a suggestion, they must turn their comment into a question. So, the times when Ken is working with Bob, the dialogue above is transformed into something along the lines of:

ACTOR: Why does my character say this?

KEN: It's because he's lying.

ACTOR: I don't understand. Why is he lying?

KEN: Because he's feeling guilty and doesn't want his wife to know what he's done.

ACTOR: Well, I didn't get that from the scene.

BOB: Let's try to re-phrase that last comment as a question. Ken, do you think the fact that he's lying could be made clearer?

KEN: I thought it was already clear from Scene Two? I mean, he virtually lays it out for the audience.

BOB: Do you think that, by this point in Act Three, Scene Two feels like a long time ago?

KEN: Hmmm… Maybe the audience needs a refresher…

ACTOR: You know what would be cool, this is just a crazy idea, but hear me out…

BOB: Hold on. Let's let Ken offer a rewrite first before we leap in with suggestions.

KEN: I'm concerned that if the husband comes out and states his subtext directly, then he is the one who comes up with the idea, instead of the wife. It makes him the active agent, when we really need to keep focus on the wife.

BOB: I can see how that can be a danger. Do you think there's a way to phrase it so that the wife comes up with the idea?

KEN: Maybe if he starts the line, but then the wife picks up on what he's saying. You know, in the way that sometimes people who are on the same wavelength...

BOB: ...complete each other's thoughts?

KEN   (*laughing*) : Yeah, like that. You know, I really, really like this idea. Then we see the wife as the one making the intuitive leap. It's important to me that the female protagonist remains the active agent of the scene.

BOB: Is there another scene where we could apply this same technique? Say Scene Two?

KEN: I was just thinking that same thing!

Under the expert coaching of the team lead (Bob, the director), the employee (Ken, the playwright) had his ideas challenged but also remained in control of the process. When it was clear to everyone but the employee that there was a problem, the other team members (the actors) were able to identify the problem without offering a solution. By asking probing questions, the group was able to uncover a more important objective that everyone else had missed (in this case, that the female protagonist should remain the focus). The employee was encouraged to think about a possible solution, and he was able to own that solution since he'd invented it. Finally, having broken the employee free of his previous thinking, it didn't take much for the Team Lead to encourage him to think about ways to apply this new solution to other, similar problems.

The C.O.A.C.H. Model is built upon the same principle. It offers a framework with general questions to elicit goals, obstacles, options and more. When you are using questions, you don't need to be an expert in every specific situation to be able to coach your team. And when dealing with an employee wearing a Hard Hat or Graduate Cap, questions are more useful tools than suggestions.

Current Situation • Outcome Desired • Actions Possible
Critical Choice • How To Be Accountable

THE C.O.A.C.H. MODEL

In the model we propose to you, C.O.A.C.H. stands for five different stages:

1. You must first describe the CURRENT situation so that you and your Hard Hat or Graduate Cap are on the same page.

2. Then you can together define the OUTCOME you desire.

3. After that, it's time to identify what ACTIONS are possible. Beware of leaping into action or settling on any one of these actions prematurely, because first...

4. You must ask CRITICAL questions about those actions that prepare your employee to make an informed choice.

5. Finally, it's time to ask your employee HOW they plan to be accountable for success.

In the following section, we'll expand on each of those stages and offer a selection of sample questions. Then, in

Act Three and Four, we'll introduce you to two more fictional leaders. We'll observe how they apply the model to conversations with Hard Hats and Graduate Caps. Before proceeding, you may wish to flip back to the Prologue and review the descriptions of Hard Hats and Graduate Caps.

Describe the CURRENT Situation

Your first task as a coach is to achieve a shared understanding of the Current Situation. This is harder than it seems, because many times you and your employees have different interpretations of the problem at hand, the state of the company's fortunes, or the objectives of the company as a whole.

If a leader and team member don't agree on the fundamentals, then conflict is bound to arise. For instance, in Act One, Raj felt that the issue at hand was that Veronique was not completing the reports properly. However, Veronique had a completely different view. She felt that the work she was doing was inconsequential and beneath her. Because this disconnect was not addressed early in their first dialogue, they were operating from different assumptions. As a result, Veronique donned her Viking headgear.

When assumptions are not fully articulated, both parties can feel unheard and frustrated. That's bad enough during the course of one interaction, but if this misunderstanding continues over weeks or months, then it can fester. One of the founders of modern psychology, Carl Jung, contended, "What you resist not only persists, but will grow in size." This insight proves true, regardless of whether we are speaking of supressed childhood trauma or a denial of reality in the workplace. Fortunately for us, Carl Jung pointed out that the reverse is equally true, "What you embrace dissolves and loses power over you." As we'll see in the examples coming up in Acts Three and Four, once a mutual understanding of the Current Situation is achieved, both parties can move forward.

Often this step is valuable in and of itself. A person confronted with a difficult workplace issue may be confused as to what is really going on or they may be overwhelmed by the situation, or they may simply not be able to see the forest for the trees. A guided conversation with a neutral third party (i.e. the coach) helps them see the situation clearly.

So how do you go about it?

Begin by asking probing questions about the current situation so you can ensure that you are both on the same page. Here is a sample list of some questions that allows you to seek out facts and find concrete examples to illustrate the current situation. As you read through the list, try to identify what is a common element to all of these questions.

Sample probing questions to
Describe the CURRENT Situation

- What is Happening now?
- What impact is the current situation having?
- On a scale of 1 to 10: how serious is the situation?
- How do you think other people at work are feeling at the moment?
- What is your biggest priority at work at the moment?
- What has gone really well for you at work recently?
- What is most important to you about your work?
- On a scale of 1 to 10: how fulfilled are you in your role?
- In which aspects of your work are you LEAST comfortable and confident?
- In which aspects of your work are you MOST comfortable and confident?
- Which aspects of your work do you avoid or shy away from?
- What do you value most about working in this organization?
- What do you think you do to enhance this organization?
- What are the major challenges facing you at work at the moment?
- What obstacles are holding you back from doing your job more effectively?
- What is most important to you about your work?
- What are you like when you are at your best at work?

What common elements in all of these questions did you uncover? Here's our answer, which may be different from yours; what stands out to us is that *each question demands a specific answer.*

Sure, it's *possible* to offer a generic response, but you can easily call it out. For example, if you ask a question like, "What do you value most about working in this organization?" you may hear "Oh, I dunno, everything…" You can press your unmanageable employee for an honest and insightful answer. In fact, digging for a better answer and refusing to let your employee off the hook is almost all you have to do in a coaching situation. (However, like everything else, that's also easier than it sounds.)

What's important at this stage is that you and your employee agree upon the current situation. That's why we think it's important that the coach digs for specifics, because it is in clarifying the details that you will help her or him get clear on what is actually happening. Be sure you and your coachee come to an agreement on this before you end this phase of questioning.

Define Desirable OUTCOMES

Once the current situation is defined, agreed upon and accepted, then you can begin to discuss the desired OUTCOME.

You may feel tempted to rush to problem solving right away. Resist this urge, even if you have limited time, if the situation is potentially dangerous or if a deadline is looming. Remember that there is a big difference between deciding to leave and knowing where to go.

Often, we want to be a hero and provide the answer to our employee if they are struggling with the question. Resist this impulse. Imagine that you are a patient at the doctor's office with a strange pain in your shoulder. How would you feel if the doctor interrupted and prescribed amputation? Wouldn't you rather she explores a few other options? Perhaps physiotherapy? Or at the very least, a manual examination to make sure that it isn't just a sprained muscle? Or maybe you'd at least like to finish your sentence?

In addition to slowing down yourself, you may need to put the brakes on your employee. A Graduate Cap or Hard Hat can be uncomfortable with not knowing the answer. Leaping to a solution, even if a part of them is unsure if it will work, makes them feel like they're standing back on solid ground and can save face.

There's another danger in moving too quickly. An employee who desires an immediate solution may have slipped on one of the hats from the first half of our book. They may have a vision of a future in which the current problematic situation has dissolved or transformed into a more positive, problem-free state, without them having to actually do anything about it. If this is the case, you'll need to put your coaching session on hold in order to have a challenge conversation with them.

Usually your team member will have put some thought into what they want to achieve and may be presenting you with one or two desired outcomes. If they're a Hard Hat, their view of what is possible may be limited by past experience and ingrained habits. They may be setting their sights too low. In this case, you need to help them stretch and imagine the full scope of what might be possible. Graduate Caps tend to face the opposite challenge. They may know there are multiple options out there, but they'll be frustrated and overwhelmed by the sheer volume of possibilities. It will be your job to help them see the forest when they are surrounded by the trees.

You can help them focus their attention by distinguishing between End Goals and Performance Goals. End Goals are reflective of the company's strategic, big picture objectives. Examples of End Goals are helping the company become a market leader in a new technology space, helping the business development team break into new markets, or influencing government policy around important issues. End Goals can be daunting for a Hard Hat because they are ambitious, require a longer time frame, and are impacted by factors outside their control. There's nothing wrong with using End Goals as inspiration but you will have to refocus their attention on manageable milestones along the way.

A Performance Goal is one that is within your control and can be measured within a reasonable time frame. For instance, if the End Goal is for your company to become a market leader in your industry, the Performance Goal your Graduate Cap agrees to, might be to increase sales by 20% a year. Your Hard Hat can think in even smaller increments such as increasing sales by 5% every quarter until they reach 20% by the end of the year.

Sample open-ended questions
that help define desirable OUTCOMES

- What goal do you want to achieve?
- What are you hoping to achieve with this goal?
- If anything was possible, what would you do?
- What do you want to achieve from this coaching session?
- Where do you see yourself in five years?
- What are the key outcomes you want to achieve in your work?
- What do you want to change?
- What do you really want?
- How can I, as your manager, get the best out of you?
- What is it that you really want to be and do?
- What are the greatest opportunities for improvement in your current role? Why?
- What would make your job even more meaningful?
- What are the top five things you'd like to do in your role?
- What would need to happen for you to improve your performance at work?
- What outcome would be ideal?
- What is most important to you about your work?
- What would you like to accomplish?

As a coach, you can play a valuable role in helping your team member expand their range of options and encourage them to explore novel ways of tackling seemingly intractable problems by asking some of the following big-picture, open-ended questions on the opposite page.

Of course, you can invent your own questions. Just ensure that they're open-ended and encourage a full, meaningful answer using the subject's own knowledge and/or feelings. It is the opposite of a closed-ended question, which encourages a short or one-word answer, like a simple "yes" or "no".

Also be sure to avoid leading questions. A leading question is one which subtly prompts the respondent to answer in a particular way. This results in false or slanted information and is just another way for you to manipulate your employee into doing what you want them to do.

Use these open-ended questions to get to a desired outcome that does more than simply address the symptoms. Strive to help them drill down and solve root causes. Don't quit until you get your employee to identify a solution or aspiration that excites them.

Once the desired outcome has been established (or re-established) then the real meat of the coaching can begin.

Identify Possible ACTIONS

Once you and your team member have agreed upon the outcome you desire, you can start to produce a list of actions that have the potential to get you there. By asking the right questions, you may get them generating several new ideas that they might not previously have identified.

This is different from brainstorming. Traditional group brainstorming consists of generating as many ideas as possible, no matter how wacky. It usually results in nothing more than a sheet of flip chart paper that gets thrown in the recycling. This is because usually one of two hazards lie in wait.

The first is The Loud Voice. Extroverts or those with authority tend to dominate brainstorming conversations to the exclusion of introverts or more junior members. We may defer to someone who is a subject matter expert or has social status or is very passionate or particularly articulate. Then we don't second-guess the idea until the meeting is over.

You may think that you won't have this problem in a one-on-one setting. However, because you're the boss, there is an inescapable power imbalance. No matter how much you try to be friendly, approachable and "one of the guys", your opinion has more weight. The result is that virtually anything you say will steer or influence the direction of the conversation. This is particularly true with a Hard Hat because, by definition, a Hard Hat has difficulty finding their bearings and is looking to you for direction. An individual wearing a Graduate Cap may be so eager to make an impact, they leap upon the first idea you suggest.

The second peril of brainstorming is the temptation to evaluate ideas as you go. We've found time and time again that critiquing ideas as soon as they appear is a soul-destroying habit that never fails to suck the oxygen out of a room. Jake

Knapp, who co-created the Google Ventures Sprint Process notes that, "These discussions are frustrating because humans have limited short-term memory and limited energy for decision-making. When we jump from option to option, it's difficult to hold important details in our heads. On the other hand, when we debate one idea for too long, we get worn out, like a judge at a baking contest who fills up on apple pie before tasting anything else[10]."

Once again, when posing questions to identify possible actions, you should focus on open-ended questions. You want to expand the horizon rather than narrow it.

We call these questions prompts because we want to remind you to prompt your team member to come up with the solution themselves. It's much wiser to brainstorm in conjunction with your team member, instead of ordering them about. Then you are allowing them to come up with solutions they can really get behind. Don't feel that you need to have all the answers. Remember, if you need to be the smartest person in the room all the time, then you're going to be the one doing all the heavy lifting all the time.

[10] Jake Knapp created the Sprint process with John Zeratsky and Braden Kowitz. The three have collected their ideas in *Sprint: How to Solve Big Problems and Test New Ideas in Just Five Days.* This quote comes from page 128.

Sample open-ended questions to identify possible ACTIONS

- What actions can you take to move things forward?
- What are your options?
- Where are you now in relation to your goal?
- What steps have you already taken towards your goal?
- What could be your first step?
- What do you think you need to do right now?
- What do you think you need to do next?
- Tell me how you're going to do that.
- Have you tackled a similar situation before?
- What else could you do?
- What will you do differently tomorrow to meet these challenges?
- What would you do if time were not an issue?
- What additional resources do you need to do your work well?
- Who else might be able to help?
- What do you need from me/others to help you achieve this?
- Who do you know who can help you do your job more effectively?
- Describe your ideal job. Tell me how it differs from what you're doing now?
- What could you do differently?

So how exactly do we go about generating and encouraging ideas? By combining two simple yet powerful words: "Yes" with "And".

The catchphrase "Yes And" comes from the world of Improvisation and came to prominence through the teachings of our fellow Calgarian Keith Johnstone who is credited with inventing Theatresports, the format that was made popular by The Second City comedy club and the TV show *Who's Line Is It Anyway?* "Yes And" has been adopted far and wide amongst actors, improvisers and artists of all sorts. It has also migrated into corporate training exercises, as a powerful tool for finding creative solutions to business problems. It has been made even more popular by Daniel Pink's book, *To Sell is Human*.

The core idea is that it's impossible to brainstorm with someone who says "no" to any and all suggestions. For example, imagine that you and your team are looking to increase market share:

THEM: Let's build a new ad campaign for that high-end product.

YOU: No, we like what we have.

THEM: Then let's reach out to existing customers and see if we can upsell them.

YOU: No, we don't want to risk losing them.

THEM: What **if we** develop a mid-priced version of the same product?

YOU: No, we don't want to confuse our brand.

Each "no" may be accompanied by a valid rationale, but it's impossible to proceed or build momentum. Moreover, the partner who is making all the offers is very quickly exhausted and abandons the exchange. If you want to see how badly this can go, just try it yourself at home with your loved one, while planning what you're going to do for the weekend and see how long it takes before your partner throws up their hands and starts packing their bags so they can leave you behind.

In the world of improvisation, a suggestion is called "an offer" and the act of throwing an idea on the table is called "making an offer". It's a useful bit of jargon because the term "offer" acknowledges the emotional cost of putting your idea out into the world. Consider the following two phrases for a moment:

- "Jackie has thrown an idea on the table."
- "Jackie has made an offer."

In which of the two scenarios are you most likely to treat what Jackie has given you with more delicacy? In which scenario has Jackie taken more emotional risk? Every time we make a proposal to our partner, be it in our personal relationship or our workplace, there's a risk that the person we trust / love / look up to / work for, may reject our idea. For many, there is an inescapable feeling that it also means they are rejecting us. Re-labelling a suggestion as an "offer" acknowledges that your teammate has given you something that is valuable and obligates you to treat it with respect even if you choose not to keep it.

A much more valuable and productive response to an offer is "yes". Many improv exercises attempt to free the creative mind by inviting one partner to make an offer, and inviting the second partner to accept that offer, no matter how outrageous. The results are often hilarious but also illuminating. Participants slowly realize how freely the discussion evolves when "yes" is the only option.

YOU: What are our options for increasing market share?

THEM: We can build a new campaign for that high-end product.

YOU: Yes.

THEM: I know that our market research says it appeals to grandparents, but I want to appeal to Millennials because it will be more fun.

YOU: Yes.

THEM: Let's use loud music and a lot of nudity in the ads.

YOU: Uh… Yes?

The exercise is often energizing and empowering. Though of course, in the world of business, an unqualified yes can lead to some very strange and unprofitable places. The fear of straying into these places can prompt a leader to revert to "no" as a knee jerk reaction to any suggestion. It's for this reason that teams often have tremendous fun at Improv in the Workplace workshops, but don't implement the behaviour when they return to the workplace.

The world of communication is even more nuanced when we realize that most people say "Yes" when they mean "No". In the world of improvisation this is revealed through the phrase "Yes But".

YOU: What are our options for increasing market share?

THEM: We can find a way to promote that high-end product to a younger demographic.

YOU: Yes but a splashy campaign would alienate our existing customers.

THEM: We could separate our audiences by launching a parallel campaign in a print media that's read only by the younger demographic.

YOU: Yes but we'd risk diluting our brand.

THEM: What if we confined our new

campaign to social media and we
used algorithms to ensure that we
were only reaching our new target
demographic.

YOU: Yes but I'm not sure that social
media will give our product the
reach to justify the expense behind
a new campaign.

The phrase "Yes But" is really just the word "No" in disguise. In this situation, any time the team member tries to be vulnerable and put a potentially valuable idea on the table, they are met with the kind of passive aggressive resistance that would make any shield-wielding Viking Helmet proud.

This is where "Yes And" proves its value as a versatile tool. It can be employed in a variety of situations to encourage team members to continue offering valuable suggestions, to build on existing ideas and/or steer team members to better ideas.

YOU: What are our options for increasing
market share?

THEM: Let's find a way to promote that
high-end product to a younger
demographic.

YOU: Yes. And we must build a campaign
that also incorporates our existing
customers.

THEM: We could find an image or idea that appeals to Millennials but also makes the existing demographic feel like they're part of the in-group.

YOU: Yes. And we need to employ a metaphor that aligns with our already resonant brand.

THEM: What if we used the tension that already exists between Millennials who have begun to adopt our product and the seniors who have been using it for years?

YOU: Yes. And we can juxtapose the senior's knowledge with wry self-deprecating humour.

THEM: Then both demographics feel like they're in on the joke.

YOU: Yes. And I'm still a little worried about diluting our brand and alienating our existing customers. I want a mockup on my desk by Tuesday so I can dispel these fears.

Even reading this dialogue and observing these completely fictional exchanges, you may see how using "Yes And" as a guiding principle is far more pleasant to experience. Its much more likely to result in an imaginative and resonant promotional campaign. The concerns that stifled creativity in the first and third exchanges are still raised and will still be addressed.

It's one thing to come up with a list of possible actions, but how do you evaluate those ideas? That's where step 4 comes in.

Ask CRITICAL Questions That Lead to a CHOICE.

In this step you can help your team member evaluate the actions you've set out together by asking CRITICAL questions that lead to a CHOICE.

This is where you can finally bring out the hard-nosed evaluator that you've been keeping in check for so long, right? Not so fast. Remember the teenager analogy we used earlier? If you are the parent of a teenager (or have ever been a teen) you'll realize the perils of offering seasoned advice on any course of action. Remember, your job as a coach is NOT to get on the playing field. You're trying to give them the tools to do it for themselves. Continue to ask probing questions that help them get to a solution.

If your employee's default setting is a Sun Hat, they may try to slip that bonnet back on when you're not looking and ask you to make the decision for you. Don't fall for it. Keep the focus on them. Don't let them put on their Viking Helmet and bully you into making the decision for them either. That's simply giving them the opportunity to return next week and tell you it's all your fault the plan didn't work out.

Of course, if you have a firm opinion of what may work, you don't need to keep completely silent. Remember the story of Theatre Director Bob White, who turns every piece of advice into a question. Begin your suggestion with the words "What would happen if?" or "What do you think is stopping you from?" or "What would you gain or lose by?" Virtually any instruction you feel inclined to give, can be replaced by a question. Once you frame it as a question, you're inviting your employee to evaluate and take ownership of the direction.

If you're uncertain of the wisdom of a course of action your team member is dead set upon and convinced of your own suggestion, then by all means listen to your instincts and issue a firm directive. But remain open to the possibility that because your team member is the one in the trenches, she may know the lay of the land better than you. Let us turn the tables on you and ask you a coaching question: what would happen if you allowed your employee to embark on a rapid prototype of her idea that doesn't involve a lot of resources and has minimal risk? Would you remain open to changing your mind? What would it take to convince you? Remember, you can always keep your own idea in your back pocket and suggest it again at your next meeting, if your team member's suggestion doesn't work out.

The main point is that you must continue to approach this phase as you have all the others: as an opportunity to create a shared vision.

Sample CRITICAL questions that lead to a CHOICE

- What has contributed to your success so far?
- What are you doing really well that is helping you get there?
- What are you NOT doing well that is preventing you from getting there?
- What are the pros and cons of your approach?
- What would happen if you did nothing?
- What have you already tried?
- What is the best way you have handled a situation like this in the past?
- How could you turn it around this time?
- On a scale of 1 to 10, what is the likelihood of your plan succeeding?
- What would be the benefits if you achieved this goal?
- If everything goes well, how will your life be different?
- What roadblocks do you expect?
- What do you think is stopping you?
- What would happen if you did that?
- What would you gain/lose by saying that?
- What's motivating you to contemplate these actions?
- Which course of action have you already decided on?
- Which option do you feel ready to act on?

Someone who comes to their own conclusions about the effectiveness of a course of action will be much more likely to commit to it over the long term.

We find that this is where some coaching models end. Having identified a way forward, most coaches leave the team member to move forward on their own, without further support. Since you're working with us, you're not done yet. We've got one more crucial step for you and your team member.

HOW to Move Forward and Be Accountable for Success

Your final, and pivotal, step is to help your team member look for ways to ensure that she or he is accountable for their success. Note that we have not said that YOU should look for ways that YOU can hold them accountable. Instead, as with every other step, your job is to help them look for ways to hold *themselves* accountable.

That said, Graduate Caps generally find it easier to create their own metrics and hold themselves accountable. Hard Hats may need greater guidance and they may need you to hold them responsible through regular meetings.

As you guide them towards building what is essentially an accountability plan, it may be useful to think of the commonly used acronym S.M.A.R.T. and urge them to set goals which are Specific, Measurable, Actionable, Realistic, Time-bound[11].

The goal should be **specific** and clear otherwise your employee may easily lose their way. Imagine that your Hard Hat comes into work a week from now, harried by the usual assortment of distractions and annoyances. Preoccupied in

[11] We know! We know! Another acronym... but its working, right?

this way, they are prone to falling back into old Sun Hat or Viking Helmet behaviour. Now imagine, at this precise moment, they see a sticky note on their computer with their accountability goals written clearly in black marker. The goal you've brainstormed should be simple enough that it refocuses their attention.

It should also be **measurable** so that you and your employee can regularly regroup and determine together how far she has progressed towards the goal. Be sure to keep your own in a file on your desk. Or, if your job requires you to be mobile, then follow the lead of Jonathan Rosenberg, co-author of, *How Google Works* who managed the design and development of Google products such as Search, Ads, Gmail, Android, Apps, and Chrome. Rosenberg keeps track of deliverables for each direct report using the notes field of the Contacts or Calendar App.

If the goal you jointly set is **actionable**, then it's far less likely that your employee will be tempted to slip back into previous patterns of Sun Hat behaviour and convince herself that the instructions were too vague for her to act on. You can ensure that a goal is actionable by using a compelling verb that accurately describes the goal. For example, "complete the recommendations section" is much better than "do that chunk". Even if you know what it means during the meeting, it loses its meaning a week later.

If you set a **realistic** target and a reasonable number of goals, then your employee won't end up overwhelmed and march back into your office with their Viking Helmet on to tell you that they're about to explode. You can ensure it's realistic by checking in with your team member and asking for confirmation. Just because *you* feel that you could accomplish these ten tasks in 48 hours, doesn't mean that *they* have the same skills, experience or capacity.

Finally, if you schedule a **time** for a follow-up meeting then you both know what's expected. We recommend meeting within the next week. Even if the goal you've set is a stretch goal with a long-time horizon, you should have broken it down into a chain of smaller, realistic performance objectives that can be acted on in succession. Review the progress on each of these stages at your check-in.

Of course, once you've scheduled a check-in, keep your word and honour the appointment. If you expect accountability from your employees, then you must model it first.

Sample questions for HOW to be accountable for success:

- When are you going to start?
- What are three actions you can take this week?
- What one small step will you take now?
- What progress will you make this week?
- How can I help?
- What is holding you back from achieving more?
- Who else can you share your plan with to help you be accountable?
- What gaps do you have in your skills to achieve your objective? How will you fill those gaps?
- How committed are you to changing?
- On a scale of 1 to 10, how committed are you to your plan? What would it take to make it a 10?
- What will you do to ensure this becomes a regular part of how you think and behave?
- What have you decided to do differently starting tomorrow?
- What does success look like?
- How can I best make you accountable for the results you want to achieve?
- When will you complete this?
- If everything goes well, how will your life be different?
- When will you evaluate your progress and how?

PLAN YOUR JOURNEY

A good way of thinking about the C.O.A.C.H. Model is to think about how you'd plan a journey. First, you'd establish what state (or province) you are currently in, by agreeing upon the current situation. Then you would decide where you and your team are going to end up by defining the ideal outcome. After that you and your travelling companions would make a map by brainstorming possible routes (or, in our case, possible actions). Together you'd chose a route by asking the kind of critical questions about the terrain that would lead to an informed choice about the direction you want to take. Once you've set out on your road trip, you likely wouldn't put your vehicle on autopilot even if you had a fancy autonomous vehicle with a GPS guiding you. One of you would act as navigator and be accountable for periodically checking landmarks against the map you've made.

If you follow the C.O.A.C.H. Model (or any coaching model for that matter) you're not just setting out on a random track, you are ensuring that all your team members are heading in the same direction. You're also making sure that they are prepared for the obstacles that they might meet on the way and that they've committed to seeing the journey through. Taking the time to plan will make the road ahead much more efficient and direct. It will save on gas too.

With that metaphor in mind, the questions we've provided can serve to facilitate the discussion. The next time you have a coaching session, take a few minutes before your colleague arrives and select three questions for each phase that strike you as relevant. Once you've selected three questions for each phase, you should have a total of 15 questions. Now take away one question for each category, meaning that you're taking away five in total and have ten left. Finally, when in the meeting, choose only one question to ask for each phase[12]. This ensures that your questions are focused, and you are being intentional in your coaching.

Some readers have found it's a bit awkward drawing the questions directly from the book. After a while, the pages are a mess of pencil marks and dog-eared pages. We've found it useful to print each question on a card, which makes shuffling through them a breeze. To make it easy for you, we've created a set of C.O.A.C.H. cards that you can order from our website, printed in the resources section at the back of this book.

Don't forget that the goal here is to have a conversation, not to follow a process. Any coaching model is a framework, especially this one. As such, it's intended to be used as a jumping-off point for a broader discussion. Remember that the goal is the dialogue and our model is only a tool by which to start and guide that conversation. The cards are useful here as well, because you move the appropriate card to the forefront, as the conversation evolves.

Sir John Whitmore, an English former race car driver turned performance coach, wrote that, "Coaching is unlocking people's potential to maximize their own performance." In short,

[12] As the conversation progresses, one of the questions you chose might be a dud. Be flexible and choose another if needed.

it's about helping your people learn and define for themselves, rather than telling them what to do. You want to foster awareness, responsibility, and self-confidence in the coachee. When dealing with Hard Hats and Graduate Caps, it is helpful to remind yourself that while you (the coach) can own the process, it's vital that the coachee owns the content of the conversation.

ACT THREE: BUILDING A PLAN TOGETHER

Managing The Fxxxing Hard Hat

In Act Three, we'll look at the Hard Hat and examine two ways that this behaviour can manifest: a dependent individual who needs to be guided by a plan or a self-directed individual who needs to be supervised. Then we'll look at a sample scenario that illustrates the Hard Hat in action. As with our previous examples, we'll see the interaction fail once, and then we'll rewind and see how the situation could be different if the C.O.A.C.H Model was applied.

As before, we'll turn to a historical incident for inspiration, in this case, from the world of international sport. We'll go a little further than we did in Act One and Act Two and look at a third scene in which we see the C.O.A.C.H. Model applied to long term career path development. As always, there are worksheets that you can either fill out in the book or, if you don't have a pen or pencil, you can use as a thought exercise.

ACT THREE, SCENE ONE

Now that you're well versed in the C.O.A.C.H. Model, let's look at a fictional coaching session in action throughout the following pages. In this section you'll meet Dan, a Project Manager for Riverside Construction.

Let's say that Dan took one of our courses *Managing The Unmanageable* about a year ago and has had so much success using the B.E.E.F. Model, that he's become a bit of an evangelist, sharing it widely amongst the supervisors that report to him, so they can use it with the foremen they supervise. Last month, Dan enrolled in our course *Coaching for Results*, where he learned the C.O.A.C.H. Model. He was able to apply the model in a series of customized scenarios with our live actors and so the model is sticking with him.

Dan is experiencing frustrations with one of his direct reports, Mario. Mario is a supervisor at Riverside Construction, who is responsible for a dozen foremen, each of whom is responsible for a small crew of between 5-10 manual labourers. Mario is experiencing challenges with one of his foremen, Jerry. Dan knows that in the past, these conversations have been a weakness for Mario. In this business, when a guy isn't pulling his weight you have to bring down the hammer. Sometimes it seems, Mario would rather lift a hammer than bring it down. At other times, Mario overcompensates and brings down the hammer too hard.

It's up to Dan to coach Mario through the five steps of the C.O.A.C.H. Model. To give their dynamic some flavour, let's also say that Mario is Dan's cousin. To really add some extra spice, we'll also make Mario the son of the owner of River-side Construction. We've consulted with several family-run firms and have discovered that it often brings a few extra complications. Let's see what this looks like.

Lights up on Dan's office. Dan sees Mario at the door and speaks without looking up.

DAN: So? How'd it go?

MARIO: Not good. It just got him all fired up. So now I got one of those - what'd'you call 'em? One of those Viking guys on my crew.

DAN: For cryin' out loud.

MARIO: Tell me about it. First, he was a lazy SOB, now he's a lazy and disrespectful SOB. I'm telling you, we're gonna have to let him go.

DAN: I've told you this a million times, Mario. You can't fire a guy just because he's a pain in the ass. Jerry's been with us for a long time and he's always pulled his weight.

MARIO: But he's NOT pullin' his weight any more, that's the point. These days he's taking two-hour lunches. He's late almost every morning. The other day when I swung by to have the talk with him, the crew was just standin' around.

DAN: What did you say to him?

MARIO: Hold on. I got my notes right here.

Mario unfolds a piece of paper

> So, I made my notes beforehand, like
> you said. I wrote everything out,
> right? So, I'd know what I was gonna
> say. See? I'm learning.

*Mario hands the paper to Dan. Silence while
Dan scans the page. Mario shifts in his seat.*

DAN   (*frowning*) :Did you read it to him
            right from the page?

MARIO: Well, I wanted to get it right, eh? I
            mean, because you told me it was so
            important to get the wording
            just so.

DAN: Show me.

DAN: What'd'ya mean?

DAN: Let's do a little role-play. I'm Jerry.

MARIO   (*grinning*) : Can I be Brad Pitt?

DAN: Don't be a clown. Just show me how
            you had this conversation.

Mario picks up the paper.

MARIO: "I wish to speak to you about your
            punctuality. It's come to my

attention from the men on your crew that you have been late returning from lunch break on several occasions. For example, this week alone, you have been late on Monday, Tuesday and Thursday (that is to say, yesterday). The effect this has on your crew is that they are inactive, which means work is falling behind, and they have to put in more overtime."

DAN: I think I see what's going on here. You're reading it like a robot, Mario.

MARIO (*sarcastically*) : Sorry, Dano. I guess I'll have to take some acting lessons from those Forum Theatre for Business guys you're so excited about.

DAN: How d' you think that made him feel, Mario? You reading to him from a piece of paper right there in front of all his guys?

MARIO: I'd think maybe it'd put the fear into him.

DAN: And how'd that work out?

MARIO: He hit the roof.

DAN: Because you pulled a power trip. You wanted to be the top dog on site, so you read him the riot act, right there in front of everybody.

MARIO: He was an hour late comin' back from lunch!

DAN: Really? An hour?

MARIO: OK, forty-five minutes. But the guys were standin' around doin' nuthin'. That's money down the drain. Dad's money. Our money.

DAN: That's why I sent you out there in the first place. To make the situation better. Not worse.

MARIO (*defensively*): I did what you told me.

DAN: I told you to have a conversation. I didn't tell you to read from a script. Use a little common sense.

MARIO: It's a little hard to use common sense when you're tellin' me what to say in every single conversation.

DAN: No I don't -

MARIO: What to say, how to say it, what order to say it in, using your stupid little Models.

DAN: The B.E.E.F. Model works.

MARIO (*pouting*): OK, College Boy.

DAN: Did it maybe ever occur to you that there's something going on? Maybe his wife's sick? Or his kid?

MARIO: Or maybe he's drinking too many beers at lunch?

DAN: Maybe. In which case we definitely need to get him off the job and into a program.

MARIO: I think maybe we just need to get him off the job.

DAN: Really? If a guy with fifteen years' service has got a problem, you're fine with just cutting him loose? Two week's severance pay and see you later?

Mario shifts uncomfortably in his seat.

MARIO: Well… no.

DAN: I should hope not. That's not the way this company works.

MARIO: No.

Silence.

DAN: You're going to go back to Jerry and you're going to have a conversation. A REAL conversation. And you're going to try to find out WHY he's got this lateness issue.

MARIO: Fine.

DAN: I need a little more than "fine"
            Mario.

MARIO: I'll have a real conversation, sir,
            and find out why Jerry's being a
            pain in the ass. Sir.

DAN: Good.

MARIO: Good.

*Mario exits, but he leaves the door open
behind him.*

Evaluation

Now that you've had the opportunity to watch a Hard Hat in action, let's analyze what we've observed and how it differs from a Viking Helmet.

1. Did Dan's coaching help or hinder the situation?

☐ Help

☐ Hinder

2. Identify three things that Dan could do to help Mario be more effective.

i. _____

ii. _____

iii. _____

3. If you had the opportunity to coach Dan on how to approach Mario about his behaviour, what is the single most important piece of advice you'd give?

_____

_____

_____

4. By the end of the dialogue how likely do you think Mario is to change?

1	2	3	4	5	6	7	8	9	10
Not Likely								Very Likely	

Well, That Could Have Gone Better

Let's compare your evaluation of Dan's coaching abilities to ours. You're bound to have thought of things that we didn't think of, and perhaps we've written some points that didn't occur to you. That doesn't make you wrong. In fact, we're curious to see what you've thought. Email us and let us know at **info@ineedtof-ingtalktoyou.com**

To begin with let's give Dan some credit and identify what he did well. First of all, Dan is not willing to fire Jerry outright, which seems to be Mario's preferred option. Dan also understands that Jerry may have deeper issues underlying his behaviour. When Mario tried to write it off as a drinking problem, Dan's first response is to get him into a program. So clearly Dan is dedicated to the development of his employees.

If only Dan had the same degree of empathy for the employee right in front of him.

Dan and Mario are family, and you can see their personal history is affecting their interaction. Their past history is never referenced directly, but it's evident in phrases that Dan uses such as "Don't be a clown", "I've told you a million times" and "Use a little common sense". Dan probably wouldn't talk like that to very many people. He's letting his personal feelings get in the way. It's clear he has a preconceived set of notions about Mario that are colouring his responses.

Dan falls prey to the very same power trip of which he accuses Mario. He jumps on the fact that Mario didn't execute the conversation with Jerry well and he's overly harsh with Mario for his failings. Many people fail to give full credit to someone who is trying to improve. If they see someone fall back on old habits once, they assume that all is for naught. When in fact, progress almost always requires incremental improvement, which is full of little setbacks. Figure 1 charts the dynamic progress of improvement in the vast majority of cases.

Dan is impatient with Mario and easily frustrated with the fact that Mario just doesn't seem to get it as easily as he does himself. Psychologists call this the "false consensus bias." It's a common perceptual bias, in which people tend to assume that the majority of other people think like they do. They over-estimate the extent to which their opinions, beliefs, preferences, values, and habits are typical. A person exhibiting false consensus bias may not think that everyone thinks like they do, but they think most people do.

This becomes dodgy when individuals with false consensus bias assume that those who do not agree with them or who think in a different fashion, are defective in some way. This is why we think the metaphor of the four hats is so powerful. As we mentioned earlier, it's far too easy to think that our "unmanageables" are defective in some way or even worse, that they are ethically unreliable because they are not doing their job.

The truth is that Mario is a typical Hard Hat; he wants to do what Dan is asking of him, he just lacks the skills. When you get down to it, whose fault is that really? Dan may have told Mario about the B.E.E.F. Model, but he hasn't shown Mario

Figure 1

How we envision change

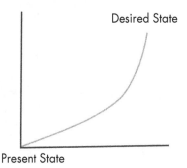

Present State

How change actually happens

Present State

how to use it. As a result, Mario hasn't integrated it into his thinking or his way of speaking. This is really the purpose behind our workshops and behind our use of the dialogues in this book. We find when participants have the opportunity to apply what they've learned in a safe environment, or watch others do so, then the learning sticks.

Dan has yet to learn what you may have already figured out; when we don't honour the genuine effort they are putting in, a Hard Hat can get easily discouraged. This is understandable. Reflect on the last time you struggled to learn a new skill that didn't come naturally and how you reacted when someone highlighted your slow progress. To be an effective coach, Dan needs to ask what other strengths and talents Mario brings to the job. He needs to identify how he can build on Mario's talents and free his blocks.

To do that, Dan needs to know what kind of Hard Hat Mario is wearing.

BRINGING DOWN THE HAMMER

Let's say you've persuaded one of your team members to re-move their Sun Hat or set aside their Viking Helmet. Now they've adopted another piece of headgear, a construction worker's yellow Hard Hat.

Your team member is now ready to roll up their sleeves, grab their tools and build a new process. They've got their cover-alls, their tool belt and their lunch pail. They've risen before the sun, stopped at Tim Horton's and parked their truck on-site. They're standing ankle deep in mud surveying the con-struction site when it dawns on them, "I haven't got a damn clue what I'm doing."

The hard-hatted individual is willing to change but does not know how or what to do to move forward. They need clear direction to overcome inertia. We can tag this person as a **yes negative**.

As their leader, you've put a lot of work into convincing them to set down their shield or sword, or into persuading them to re-focus their attention from the paperback or dragging them out of the Tiki Bar. After that superhuman effort, you may have forgotten there's another step. You may have even collapsed from exhaustion after the effort of hauling them back onside and now you need to take one or two days off. Plus coaching the other less recalcitrant members of the team is a relief by comparison.

But now the Hard Hat has marched into the construction site office, plopped themselves in the chair opposite your desk, and you can't ignore them.

The good news is they're usually asking for one of two things: a set of blueprints or a foreman.

The Hard Hat Looking for Blueprints

This individual is willing to be somewhat self-directed as long as they have a plan. But not just any plan. It has to be a detailed, step-by-step schematic, or they won't trust themselves to follow it. A high-level overview won't work for them. There are too many variables to sort through and too many opportunities or missteps for them to be comfortable with that 30,000 foot view. You'll find this person saying things like:

1. "Can you help me figure out where to start?"

The Hard Hat is not a self-starter or if they were at one point, a succession of poor or indifferent managers has beaten or bled it out of them. It's important to keep an open door and give this individual lots of support as they move along. If you give them the first few steps, they may be able to identify the third and fourth steps on their own. Then they can return to you for further instructions once they get blocked.

2. "I've got an idea, do you think it's OK for me to try it?"

The Hard Hat has learned that initiative is more often punished than rewarded. They may have learned this firsthand by making mistakes and suffering the wrath of their superiors, or they may have observed that those who stick their necks out soon find their head in their hands. You need to reassure them they're taking the right steps. Most importantly, they need to trust that you've got their back.

3. "What are my targets?"

Hard Hats who overcome these first two barriers to inertia and start moving may find themselves unsure of how far they're expected to go. They're not in a position to, or they're not giving themselves the authority to, set those targets for themselves. Give them clear goals and objectives initially. Coach towards the point where they can set those goals for themselves.

4. "What if we did it this way?"

After your Hard Hat works his or her way through the first few blocks, they may begin brainstorming with you. Even better, they may come up with ideas on their own. But you'll find that uncertainty means they need validation to proceed. If you think their idea is workable, then praise them for their instincts or analytical thinking. If their idea needs work, don't tear it apart. Praise them for their initiative and build on their idea.

Even once they receive the blueprint, you can't always rely on the Hard Hat to move forward under their own steam. There is always the risk that, having taken the first or second step, they'll think it's OK to return to the beach. You'll need regular check-ins to ensure they don't slip back into past behaviour.

The Hard Hat Looking for a Foreman

A Hard Hat who's truly engaged and self-aware, will come to you seeking guidance with specific questions. You'll often find a less self-aware Hard Hat, acting inappropriately by storming into your office and making demands instead. They may feel frustrated with their own inability to tackle the situation, another individual or their own shortcomings. In these cases, they're likely looking to blame external forces and turning to you to solve it for them. This kind of Hard Hat conduct can be mistaken as Viking Helmet with Sword behaviour but take heart. A Hard Hat looking for a Foreman is seeking you out, and that's a crucial difference. They picture you as an ally not an enemy. They are paralyzed with indecision and it's causing them frustration. They may begin by taking it out on you, but they can be easily refocused on the issue at hand.

1. "I don't know where to start."

This statement is often accompanied by a defeatist tone and a gesture of despair. You may find yourself disheartened because the Hard Hat needs someone to hold their hand through every step. Don't forget, they've come to you instead of slipping back to the Tiki Bar or putting on their Viking Helmet, and that's a VERY good thing.

2. "I have a few ideas but no one will let me try any of them."

You may not hear the words over the loud whine that accompanies them. A newly minted Hard Hat may take a while to shed their old practices and may still be in the habit of blaming others. At least they have ideas. Build on these notions. Find ways to remove obstacles in their path.

3. "You need to give me some direction."

This statement contains a high degree of blame. You may even hear tinges of their Viking Helmet. It's easier to point the finger at someone else than to admit that the only one holding us back is ourselves. Keep your door open for them. If you try to bar the door, they're going to return with a battering ram and a few fellow Vikings. No one wants those visitors.

4. "Just tell me how you want me to do it."

The last refuge of the frustrated Hard Hat is often a plea for a firm hand. It may be tempting to give them what they want, but if you do, you'll be micro-managing them for the rest of your tenure. Remember that if you give a man a fish, you feed him for a day. If you teach a man to fish, then you feed him for a lifetime.

A Hard Hat can be a bit frustrating at times because they require monitoring. However, this is a good employee to have because they can be coached. There is an opportunity here to be creative with them and to brainstorm together for a solution.

Evaluation

1. Flip back to Act Three, Scene One in which Dan debriefed with Mario. In your opinion was Mario:

- The Hard Hat looking for Blueprints?
- The Hard Hat looking for a Foreman?

2. List three behaviours you observed which convinced you of this.

i. _____

_____

ii. _____

_____

iii. _____

_____

Recognizing the Hard Hat in Your Workplace

Having read an overview of Hard Hat behaviour, take some time now to reflect on your own workplace. Think about your own team or, if you don't have a team, consider your co-workers or a group you've worked with previously. Do you have (or have you had) an individual wearing a Hard Hat on your team? Do you have more than one?

1. What behaviours do you see this person demonstrating that would indicate they are wearing a Hard Hat?

_____

_____

Which of the above are looking for blueprints? Which are looking for a foreman?

2. What phrases do you hear this person saying that would indicate they are wearing a Hard Hat?

_____

_____

3. What impact does their behaviour have on others in the workplace?

_____

_____

4. On a scale of 1-10 how serious is this?

1	2	3	4	5	6	7	8	9	10
Not Serious								Very Serious	

ACT THREE, SCENE TWO

Let's give Dan a do-over, just as we have with Raj in Act One, and Kendra in Act Two. By rewinding and taking a second look at the same scene, we can see how Dan can bring out the best in Mario through the C.O.A.C.H. Method.

Lights up. Dan reviews his notes from his last meeting with Mario. There aren't many, just a few comments about Jerry being late that he'd scribbled in the notebook, but it's enough to bring back the gist of the conversation about Jerry's tardiness and his increased insubordination. Dan sets the notes to one side and pulls the deck of C.O.A.C.H. cards out of his drawer. He sorts the five suits and scans through them for questions that seem applicable to the situation. It isn't hard to find two or three for each stage. He lays them out on the desk and reads through them.

Pardon the interruption.

Before you read through Dan's attempt at coaching Mario and see what questions he's selected, let's see how you would apply the C.O.A.C.H. Model if you were in his shoes. Use the worksheet on the following page as if you were Dan preparing to speak to Mario. If you have purchased the C.O.A.C.H. cards in conjunction with this book, then it may be easier for you to use the cards to sort through the questions as Dan has done. Otherwise flip back to the Intermission and scan each list of suggested questions for each of the five C.O.A.C.H. stages. Imagine you are Dan and select three questions for each of the five steps that you would ask Mario. Then read the scene and note the differences.

Preparing for a Coaching Conversation

Describe the **CURRENT** situation.

1. _____
2. _____
3. _____

Define the **OUTCOME** you desire.

1. _____
2. _____
3. _____

Identify what **ACTIONS** are possible.

1. _____
2. _____
3. _____

Ask **CRITICAL** questions that lead to making an informed **CHOICE**.

1. _____
2. _____
3. _____

Ask **HOW** they plan to be accountable for success.

1. _____
2. _____
3. _____

Now take away one question for each category. This ensures that your questions are focused, and you are being intentional in your coaching.

Lights up. Mario knocks on the door. Dan gathers up the cards and sets them to one side, and invites him to sit down.

DAN: So? How'd it go?

MARIO: Not good. It just got him all fired up. First, he was lazy, now he's lazy and disrespectful.

DAN: On a scale of 1 to 10, how serious is the situation?

MARIO: Pretty damn serious, Dan!

DAN: On a scale of 1 to 10?

MARIO: Ten. No, well, eight, I guess.

DAN: So, it's serious, but not kill-the-company-serious?

MARIO: I guess not.

DAN: What did you say to him?

MARIO: I got my notes right here.

unfolds a piece of paper

I made my notes beforehand, like you said. See? I'm learning.

DAN: You are. You're really putting in an effort. I know it's not easy for you, so I admire it even more.

MARIO: Thanks. I guess.

DAN: Did you have this talk in private? Or right there in front of all his guys?

MARIO: Well, I was gonna talk to him in the trailer or in the truck, but when I got there, there was no Jerry any where. Just his guys standin' around. This was about an hour after lunch.

DAN: An hour? Really?

MARIO: Well, close enough.

DAN: Let's not be close enough. If this escalates, and the union gets involved, we're going to need to be specific. Was it an hour after lunch?

MARIO: Um... More like forty-five minutes.

DAN: Good to know. But still unacceptable.

MARIO: I know! That's money down the drain. Dad's money.

DAN: How did you feel about that?

MARIO: I got kind of wound up.

DAN: How wound up?

MARIO: I didn't lose it on him, if that's what you're asking. I read right from the paper.

DAN: And how'd that work out?

MARIO: He hit the roof.

DAN: Any idea why?

Silence. Mario shifts in his seat.

How do you think that made him feel? You reading to him from a piece of paper right there in front of everybody?

MARIO: Probably not good.

DAN: Tell me what impact the current situation is having.

MARIO: He's costing us money.

DAN: Is that what makes it an eight?

MARIO: And he blew up at me, in front of the other guys. So that's undermining my authority.

DAN: So, undermining your authority is what makes it an eight?

MARIO: Maybe it's not an eight. Seven.

DAN: How do you think other people on the crew are feeling at the moment, after seeing the blow up?

MARIO: Well, it's not like they couldn't see

it coming.

DAN: So, the fact that you had a talk with him, in front of the crew, what's the impact of that?

MARIO: Probably... the guys like to see that things are fair, right? They can't get away with stuff like that and they see that Jerry can't either.

DAN: Right. So, do you think you earned their respect a bit?

MARIO: (*proudly*) : Yeah. I guess I did.

DAN: How serious is the situation? Still a seven?

MARIO: Maybe a five.

DAN: I guess the situation's not as serious as we thought when you first came in?

MARIO: I guess not.

Mario visibly relaxes a bit.

DAN: OK, so what are our options?

MARIO: Fire his ass.

DAN: Ok, that's one, but we just agreed it's not the best option. What do you want to change?

MARIO: I want him to change his attitude.

DAN: What would that look like?

Mario thinks about this for a moment.

MARIO: He'd stop fighting me on every little thing. We'd work together on the schedule and stuff. He'd bring some ideas to the table for a change. He'd maybe tell me when he needs some more supplies instead of waiting for me to figure it out all the time. Like I used to do for you when you were my Super.

DAN: That seems like a good thing to aim for. Can you give him a few examples?

MARIO: I'd say, "Jerry, you can't rely on me to know when you need another load of rebar or whatever. You're the one on the ground. You gotta keep an eye on your supplies and you gotta think ahead more."

DAN: That's good. What else could you do?

MARIO: Uh… I can point out that he's due for a raise this year.

DAN: Yes. Can you give him a few examples of what he needs to do? Make it concrete, so there's no mis taking it?

MARIO: "Jerry you've got seventeen years

with the company. Ten as a foreman. You know you're due for a raise this year, right? But I gotta tell ya, you ain't gonna get the raise you're due at the rate your goin'. But if you pull up your socks, show some leadership for a change, then together we can make a case to Dan that you deserve an increase."

DAN: How do you feel about that?

MARIO: Pretty OK.

DAN: What do you think is the chance of success if you have that conversation that we just did? On a scale of 1 to 10.

MARIO: Maybe an 8?

DAN: What do you need to do right now?

MARIO: I'm gonna have to go talk to him again but this time, just him and me, without all his guys around.

DAN: What do you think is stopping you?

MARIO: I just don't want to. The last time he went all ape shit.

DAN: You've already said what you're going to do differently. So, do you think it's going to blow up again?

MARIO: Maybe. No. Probably not.

DAN: So? What do to you think is stopping you?

MARIO: I guess my pride.

DAN: Are you willing to let your pride put this guy out of work? When he's got a family and three kids and a mortgage?

Mario looks shocked.

MARIO: Jesus Dan!

DAN: Are you?

MARIO: Not when you put it like that.

DAN: When are you going to start?

MARIO: Tomorrow. I'm going to let him cool off overnight. The 24-hour rule.

DAN: So, when tomorrow?

MARIO: Before quitting time.

DAN: By when?

MARIO: Argh! Before lunch ok?

DAN: You're not going to just let this second conversation slide, are you?

MARIO: Hey, who do you think you're dealing with here?

Dan cocks an eyebrow at Mario.

Ok, Ok, don't look at me like that. I won't let it slide.

DAN: On a scale of 1 to 10, how committed are you to having this second conversation next week?

MARIO: Actually, all joking aside, I think I'm pretty committed. Like a nine. If he shapes up, I think that talking about the possibility of a raise will get him engaged again. So, I'm pretty into that.

DAN: Let me know how it goes.

MARIO: I will.

DAN: And let's check in next week. See how he's measuring up.

MARIO: All right.

Mario heads for the door, stops and turns around.

Hey College Boy? Thanks.

Evaluation A (Dan)

Now that you've had the opportunity to watch the C.O.A.C.H. Model in action, let's analyse what we've observed.

First, let's take a look at Dan:

1. On a scale of 1–10 how successful do you feel Dan was in coaching Mario?

1   2   3   4   5   6   7   8   9   10
Not Successful   Very Successful

2. Re-read Act Three, Scene Two looking just at Dan's lines. Try to mark out the points when Dan is:

- describing the CURRENT situation.
- defining the OUTCOME.
- identifying what ACTIONS are possible.
- asking CRITICAL questions about those actions to prepare Mario to make an informed choice.
- asking Mario HOW he plans to be accountable for success.

3. Compare Dan's questions with the ones you chose before you read the scene. Who chose better questions?

☐ Me
☐ Dan

4. Why did Dan choose to ask the questions he did?

_____

_____

5. What would have happened if you'd asked your questions instead?

_____

_____

6. What else could Dan have done that would have helped matters?

_____

_____

_____

_____

_____

Evaluation B (Mario)

Now let's take a moment to consider Mario:

1. How did Mario respond to Dan's more focused approach? Can you point out three specific moments when Mario acted differently than he did in Scene One?

i. _____

ii. _____

iii. _____

2. If you feel Mario behaved differently this time around, why do you think that was the case?

_____

_____

_____

3. How likely do you think Mario is to take the necessary action with Jerry?

1   2   3   4   5   6   7   8   9   10

Not Likely   Very Likely

4. What support do you think Mario now needs from Dan?

_____

_____

_____

Coaching the Coach

The dialogue with Dan and Mario is based on many hours of workshops and feedback from the field. However, there is no right or wrong way to proceed. What might work for Dan might not work for you. You work in a different environment from Dan, perhaps in a different industry, and you may not work with family members. That's why the worksheets are so important; better to make mistakes on paper than in the real world.

So, if you haven't completed those worksheets to determine how well you think Dan did with Mario, go back and review them now before we compare notes.

Dan asked a lot of questions. If you go through the sample dialogue and compare the number of questions Dan asks to the statements he makes, you'll find that the questions outnumber the answers by five to one. Each of Dan's questions are drawn from the lists we've provided, and they were uttered in the exact order of the five phases of the C.O.A.C.H. Model. Dan doesn't have to announce when he's moving from one phase to another, because Mario doesn't know (or care) that there are five phases. In fact, Dan probably couldn't tell himself when he moved from one phase to another because he was just trying to surf the natural flow of the conversation. The C.O.A.C.H. Model is a guide, not a rigid process. When you have the opportunity to implement the C.O.A.C.H. Model yourself, try to follow Dan's example and move organically from one phase to another.

A number of the questions Dan applies are intended to get specific about details. He says this is in case the issue escalates, and the union gets involved, but getting clear on the facts is also good for Mario. Dan asked Mario several times to quantify how serious the situation was using a scale of 1 to 10. Note how Mario gives more positive results each time. We find asking someone to put a number on an emotionally charged incident, allows them to move away from an emotional response and give a more objective analysis.

Dan is much better during Scene Two at appreciating that Mario is putting in the effort. This doesn't mean he's going easy on Mario or letting him off the hook. Note how shocked Mario is when Dan points out to him that he might be putting a family man out of a job to save his pride. Mario wisely decides to implement the 24-hour rule before returning to the conversation with Jerry (more of us who send emails should observe this 24-hour cooling period). Dan senses that Mario might be using this cooling period to get out of following up on the conversation, so he presses Mario for a commitment by asking him for an exact date and time.

You may have observed that Scene Two, is considerably longer than Scene One. If you integrate the C.O.A.C.H. Model into your work, you may also find that these conversations take longer. That's OK. Be prepared to set aside the time. It's worth the investment to develop conversations that are less emotionally draining and more productive.

Dan is able to relate so well to Mario because he has a good deal of experience in the construction industry. Some of us can end up in industries with which we are not personally familiar. A common accusation in these instances is that, "You don't know what it's like on the ground." As long as you're relying on using probing questions to draw out the wisdom in the employee, an outsider's perspective can be beneficial.

Since Dan and Mario share an Italian background, let's take some advice from one of the most successful Italian football coaches in the history of the sport. Arrigo Sacchi was the first coach of an Italian major league soccer club who had not played professionally at an elite level himself, and he took a lot of flak for it.

JOCKEYS AND HORSES

Sacchi looked across the football pitch of the A C Milan practice field as his players jogged half-heartedly. His employees were following his instructions to the letter, but for all the effort they were putting into the drill, they might as well be laying on the grass with their jerseys bunched behind their head to make a comfortable pillow. He sighed and looked up at the executive lounge. He couldn't see anyone through the smoked glass, but he knew the CEO was there because he'd seen the Lamborghini in the car park. He sneaked a glance over his shoulder at the figure hiding in the bushes. At first he didn't see much of anything and wondered if the corporate spy had packed it in and gone home. Then he saw one of the bushes sway slightly, even though there was no breeze. He tried to supress a smile. That kid was no James Bond.

*Sacchi blew the whistle and waved the players in. His relatively short career as a premier league coach was about to get a whole lot shorter if he didn't figure out how to coach this team. He pointed angrily at the straggling players. "Hurry up!" he shouted, "I need to F**xxx**ing talk to you!"*

Three months ago, Sacchi had been at the pinnacle of his career. His provincial team had such a good record they were bumped up a division. When his phone rang, he recognized the voice of Silvio Berlusconi, the owner of A C Milan, immediately because the media replayed the phrase Berlusconi used to describe Sacchi repeatedly, "A Mr. Nobody from the provinces."

For some reason Sacchi still could not fathom, when Berlusconi asked him out for lunch, he'd said yes. When that delicious meal was complete, Berlusconi ordered them each a fine cognac, kicked back in his seat and offered Sacchi the job of coaching A C Milan in the upcoming season for more money than Sacchi had ever seen in his life.

Sacchi hummed and hawed and asked many more questions, but his mind was made up in that moment. As Sacchi prepared to stand, Berlusconi held up a finger. "Success," he warned "will be measured with silverware." Suddenly, despite the champagne and cognac, Berlusconi looked stone cold sober. "The kind that I can place on my mantelpiece and show off to the President. You have three years to bring me the cup."

Sacchi looked him in the eye, "Three years is too long."

Contracts had been signed, notices given, desks cleaned out and now, three months later, Sacchi was facing two distinct organizational cultures that formed a rough semi-circle in front of him on the pitch. On his left, four defenceman who had formed the backbone of the Italian national team, including the famous superstars Maldini and Baresi. On the right, the mercurial talent of three Dutchman, Gullit, Rijkaard and Van Basten. The media had been talking all month about the unlikelihood of a successful forced marriage between the defensive solidity of the Italians and the total football style of the Dutch.

"I must be getting old. Can anyone remind me how many minutes of football I've played?"

Silence.

"It's not a rhetorical question. I know you've read the papers. Seen the news. How many minutes of professional football have I played?"

"None."

"And that bugs the shit out of you, doesn't it Maldini?"

Maldini shrugged. "You don't know what it's like. You've never played The Beautiful Game."

Arrigo shrugged in return, "I didn't realise that to be a jockey you had to be a horse first."

Silence hung over the pack. After a moment Maldini's guffaw broke the tension.

Sacchi blew his whistle and the team took the field. He joined them in the centre of the pitch, but he left the ball on the sidelines.

"Rijkaard, pretend you have the ball."

"Pretend?"

"I call this 'Shadow Play'. I want you to focus on the shape of the game and on shape only. The opposition centre-backs are man-marking Baresi, see that?"

"Ja! There's space in behind."

Out of the corner of his eye Arrigo saw a movement in the bushes. He was certain it was the opposition team's Talent

Scout. "Let him watch," he muttered under his breath.

When the Talent Scout who sat in the damp bushes that afternoon, reported that Sacchi had the players practicing drills *without* a ball, the opposing team's manager assumed the spy had gone crazy from too many cold afternoons in the bushes. Even Belusconi, watching from his box that afternoon, was unnerved by the unorthodox approach.

The team played their first match that Sunday. AC Milan won handily. With Sacchi's ongoing coaching, questioning and cajoling the players, who bought into the system, the team continued to dominate for the rest of the season. During Arrigo Sacchi's four years at the helm, AC Milan won eight titles, including a Scudetto, back-to-back European Cups and two Intercontinental Cups. Sacchi left AC Milan to coach the Italian national team, ultimately coming within inches of winning the World Cup. His team lost only because of a shoot-out. According to Omar Saleem of *These Football Times*[13], in just a decade, the former shoe seller, "Transformed the landscape of Italian football and took Milan from perennial underachievers to Europe's most powerful club side. And in doing so, he became the greatest 'Mr Nobody' in managerial history."

[13] This quote, and much of the background for our imagined story, comes from the online blog These Football Times, for the serious fan of "real football". *Arrigo Sacchi: The Greatest Nobody Of All Time*, by Omar Saleem, 11/19/2015.

Evaluating Your Own Hard Hat

Have you always been coachable? Being coachable means being open to feedback.

1. Has there ever been an occasion when you have not been open to feedback or took feedback personally?

_____

_____

_____

2. Were you wearing your Sun Hat on the beach or in the Tiki Bar? What behaviours did you demonstrate?

_____

_____

_____

3. If you had the opportunity to go back in time and coach your old boss on how to call you out on your behaviour, what is the one piece of advice you'd give her/him?

_____

_____

_____

4. Was there a time when you were VERY coachable? What did you or others do that made you open to receiving feedback?

_____

_____

_____

Coaching Someone On and Managing Them Out

Arrigo Sacchi's comment that one doesn't need to have been a horse to be a jockey, is one of Russell's favourites. It reinforces the point that you can coach anyone to excel in their job, even if you have little first-hand knowledge of the mechanics of the industry. What's necessary, is the knowledge of how to motivate people, how to work with them to unlock their existing expertise and a structure to shape the conversation.

Arrigo Sacchi was a highly successful, if at times controversial, and outspoken figure in sports, and he was never shy about holding his team accountable even as he coached them to be their best. He was meticulous, with an obsessive attention to detail and if a player wasn't the right fit for his team, he didn't hesitate to let them go.

Sometimes when you are coaching someone, you discover that their best interests are not the same as the company's best interests. Perhaps they hate their job and they're creating a toxic work environment. Possibly the job that they're currently in doesn't match their skill level or maybe they're just not interested in the work.

Business sense would suggest that you order them to pull up their socks, provide training to develop the needed competencies and coach them until they can at least offer passable performance, but will they ever really excel in this role? How is this creating a humane workplace?

Maybe you need to do them a favour and just fire them.Or, is it best for everyone to find them a better fit within the company?

ACT THREE, SCENE THREE

Let's imagine that over the past six months, Dan has been taking an active interest in his cousin Mario. During that time, Dan began to see that it wasn't Mario who was failing to bring the skills he needed to the job, but Dan who was failing to bring the job to Mario's skills.

Lights up on a Sports Bar. Dan and Mario are sitting side by side watching AC Milan on the television. The crowd groans in unison and Mario throws up his hands. Dan smiles. He hasn't seen Mario relaxed and smiling like this for a few years. And the more he thinks about it the sadder he feels. He sets his beer on the table and gets Mario's attention.

DAN: Can I ask you a question?

MARIO: Dano, you're always asking me questions these days.

DAN: Yeah, whatever. Seriously. What obstacles are holding you back from doing your job more effectively?

MARIO: It's hard to keep track of all the loose ends. You know how you're always telling me I'm late with the paperwork, and half the time it's incomplete? I'm not really a details guy.

DAN: Why is that?

MARIO: I know, I know, you tell me I gotta pay more attention.

DAN: Forget what I tell you. Why's your paperwork late and incomplete?

MARIO: Cause there's only so many hours in a day.

DAN: Bull. We give you an extra half hour at the beginning and end of the day to finish it, right?

MARIO: Cause I hate it, I guess.

DAN: So, you're avoiding it because it's the thing you like least?

MARIO: I know, it's stupid.

DAN: It's not stupid. It's human nature. Tell me this, what are you like when you are at your best at work?

MARIO: When I'm at my best? I get my job done. Things are running smoothly. The equipment's all in the right place at the right time.

DAN: All that's great, but that's about STUFF Mario. When are YOU at your best?

MARIO: Like personally? When you're off my back.

DAN: What do you think you do to enhance this organization?

MARIO: I think I relate pretty well with the guys on the front line. Apart from Jerry, but even that's coming along.

DAN: So, you like spending time with the guys?

MARIO: Remember when we were in high school framing up those condos? You hated it. But me, I loved it from the get-go. Remember?

DAN: Yeah, I do. So, you hate the paperwork and you like getting your hands dirty?

MARIO: That's about the size of it.

DAN: And you don't do the paperwork, because you'd rather be doing the real work?

MARIO: I know, I know, I'll focus on the paperwork.

DAN: That's not really what I'm driving at. A supervisor never touches a hammer. Why'd you take the job?

MARIO: Because you told me to. You and Dad.

DAN: So, you're doing a job you hate because your Dad told you to?

MARIO: It's a family company. I'm part of the family. That's just the way it is.

DAN: What would make your job even more meaningful?

MARIO: Less paperwork.

DAN: Not what would make your job less of a pain in the ass. What would make your job more meaningful? Not to Uncle Vito. To you.

MARIO: More time with the guys, I guess.

DAN: What are the top 5 things you like to do in your role?

MARIO: I like finding solutions to problems. And the inside work. I like the finishing, when the whole picture comes together, and the building starts to finally look like a house. But that's when Martin's team shows up and I move on to the next job.

DAN: Where do you see yourself in five years?

MARIO: More of the same, I guess. I mean, what else is there? Keep the family business running.

DAN: That sounds miserable Mario.

MARIO: What do you mean?

DAN: You just finished telling me that
           you hate everything about your job:
           the paperwork, driving around all
           day, coming down hard on the
           foremen when you need to. All the
           stuff you do like, you don't get to
           do anymore. When I ask you where
           you see yourself in the next five
           years, you tell me you'll be doing
           more of the stuff you hate.

*Silence. Mario looks into his beer and avoids
Dan's eyes.*

           Let's try looking at it another way.
           Describe your ideal job.

MARIO: I don't know what you want me
           to say.

DAN: Humour me.

MARIO: Remember when we used to do the
           whole project, from start to finish?
           I miss that part. I remember this
           one time, I was doing this granite
           counter, nobody did them back then,
           so it was hard to find and super
           expensive, so I had to be real
           careful putting it in. Then the
           family showed up, out of the blue.
           She didn't quite know what to make
           of it when she saw the counter. It

was covered in grout, so it didn't look like anything special. I got some water, cleaned it off, lickety-split, so it shined black. The look on her face. Like she'd just seen her baby daughter's face for the first time or something.

Silence.

That. I wanna do that.

DAN: What would happen if you did that?

MARIO: I would be so much happier.

DAN: What are the pros and cons?

MARIO: I'd probably get bumped back down to foreman. But that's OK. I don't care if I'm not a supervisor anymore.

DAN: It's a pay cut.

MARIO: Yeah but, it's also shorter days. Mary would like that. So would the kids.

DAN: What roadblocks do you expect?

MARIO: Dad.

DAN: Why?

MARIO: It's like a demotion. He wants me to move up, not down.

DAN: He wants you to be happy.

MARIO: He wants me to be him. Geez… Look at me. I'm forty-five and I'm worried about what my Dad thinks.

DAN: I'll back you up. Want me to go with you when you tell him?

MARIO: No. I think I can manage.

DAN: What are three things you can do this week?

MARIO: Talk to Martin first. Make sure he wants me on his team. Then Dad. I don't think there's three things, is there?

DAN: You missed someone.

MARIO: Who?

DAN: Your wife?

MARIO: Oh, yeah, right.

DAN: If everything goes well, how will your life be different?

MARIO: No more paperwork! Seriously, I'd actually be doing something I like, and I'd probably do a better job too.

Evaluation

Now that you've had the opportunity to watch the C.O.A.C.H. Model in action, as Dan Coaches Mario out, let's analyze what we've observed.

1. On a scale of 1–10 how successful do you feel Dan was in coaching Mario?

1   2   3   4   5   6   7   8   9   10
Not Successful   Very Successful

2. Re-read Act Three, Scene Three, looking just at Dan's lines. Try to mark out the points when Dan is:

- describing the CURRENT situation.
- defining the OUTCOME.
- identifying what ACTIONS are possible.
- asking CRITICAL questions about those actions to prepare Mario to make an informed choice.
- asking Mario HOW he plans to be accountable for success.

3. Why did Dan choose to ask the questions he did?

_____

_____

_____

_____

_____

Now let's take a moment to consider Mario:

1. How likely do you think Mario is to take action with a career shift?

1   2   3   4   5   6   7   8   9   10
Not Likely   Very Likely

2. What support do you think Mario now needs from Dan? Or from the organization?

_____

_____

_____

_____

_____

_____

Coaching From Anywhere

In Dan's first conversation in Act Three, Scene One, he was frustrated by Mario allowing his personal relationship to get in the way. His history with Mario was a limitation, preventing him from seeing the situation clearly and allowing him to make assumptions about Mario's ability to fulfill his responsibilities. However, once Dan shifted his focus to being a coach, his personal relationship with Mario became a strength allowing empathy to anchor the conversation. As a result, we saw Mario respond positively.

We also saw how Dan was able to apply the C.O.A.C.H Model to the conversation. Interestingly, Dan didn't have to be clever or disguise what he was doing for fear that Mario would feel he was "being facilitated". The fact that there was a structure, helped provide Mario with an understanding that there were boundaries and that he was being led somewhere productive.

In Act Three, Scene Three, Dan doubled down on his personal relationship with Mario. The personal history which had been kryptonite in Scene One, became a super-strength in Scene Three, allowing Dan to coach Mario into what can (hopefully) be a more fulfilling career choice within the same organization.

As Dan and Mario's third dialogue has shown, coaching conversations can happen anywhere; in the office, in the break room and after official work hours. What's important is the care with which the leader approaches the coaching conversation. Dan has shown that a leader can care about their employee and still offer tough love that helps lead to a breakthrough realization.

SUMMARY

An employee wearing a Sun Hat is both a joy and a pain. Just because they're ready to work doesn't mean that you can spend any less time with them. In fact, they may demand more of your time and attention. This may feel like you're holding their hand or doing their thinking for them, but you need to think of it like a long-term investment.

The individual wearing a Hard Hat can be grouped into two broad categories:

- The Hard Hat looking for blueprints.
- The Hard Hat looking for a foreman.

As we've said about every model we offer, these are not strict categories. An individual may be wearing a Hard Hat but if they don't get the blueprints they need (or if the plan is not properly explained to them), they may retreat to the Tiki Bar in confusion or put on a Viking Helmet out of spite.

The "false consensus bias" in which people tend to assume that the majority of other people think like they do, is common. This becomes an issue when someone assumes that those who do not agree with them or who think in a different fashion are defective in some way.

The lines between personal and work relationships can get blurred, especially when family is involved. In these cases, it's hard to maintain objectivity. It's important to look at how you are treating a family member and ask yourself if you would treat other members of your team the same way. If not, why not?

If you integrate the C.O.A.C.H Model into your work with teams, you may also find that these conversations take longer. That's OK. Be prepared to set aside the time. It's worth the investment to develop conversations that are less emotionally draining and more productive.

ACT FOUR: THE WIND-UP TOY

Managing The F**xxx**ing Graduate Cap

In Act Four, we'll take a look at the Graduate Cap, the final in our paradigm of un-manageable employees. Unlike previous iterations, this employee is "unmanageable" not because they are unwilling to do their job, but because they are too eager.

The Graduate Cap often comes in two versions:

☐ The Grad Student who has learned from work and life and has the confidence to take initiative.

☐ The PhD who has mastered their field, who has too much confidence and thinks they know everything.

If not properly supervised, the Graduate Cap can go down a rabbit hole which is not aligned to strategy or can even "go rogue" and turn into a maverick.

As we have before, we'll look at a sample scenario that illustrates the Graduate Cap in action. We'll turn to a historical incident for inspiration. Since leaders may en-counter a Graduate Cap who is not a direct report and over whom they don't have influence, we'll look at two useful models: Four Directions of Influence and Power Bases.

Along the way there are a few worksheets that you can either fill out in the book or, if you don't have a pen or pencil, you can use as a thought exercise.

THE DARK SIDE OF THE EMPLOYEE WE ALL WANT

It's easy to forget that high performing employees come with their own issues. Sometimes when we are striving to control an outburst by a Viking Helmet or struggling to move a Sun Hat out of complacency, all we want is someone who will just do the job. We ache for the employee to whom we can give vague marching orders, and who will return from the battle with the prize.

We call this person **yes positive**. In fact, "Yes And" is a common phrase you'll hear from this individual: "Yes, that's a great idea AND I can't wait to get started." This is the employee we all want to have! Finally, someone who is starting to deliver high performance. Now we can delegate, sit back and relax. Not only are they coachable, they're like a wind-up toy. You can gear them up, let them go and focus on your own work.

However, those of us who are of a certain age will recall, most wind-up toys chatter along delightfully for a few moments, but end up thrashing against the baseboard or traipsing right off the edge of the table.

We find two common types of individuals wearing the Graduate caps: The Grad Student and the PhD.

The Grad Student

The Graduate Cap who is a Grad Student has learned from work and life and is ready to take initiative and earn your trust through such phrases as:

1. "I'm going to do this."
They're eager to take on new challenges and they persist through obstacles, distractions and lulls. Change doesn't frighten them, it energizes them.

2. "I'll do it on this schedule."
They set their own timelines. They're comfortable with processes, workflow and Gantt charts. They will take existing templates and bend them to new purpose, ensuring they account for every detail.

3. "Leave it with me. I'll report back at our next meeting."
They offer their own accountability measures. You won't need to follow up with them, because they'll be back on your doorstep with the finished product / report / plan before you have the chance.

4. "I know we can make that goal but how can we achieve even MORE?"
They're anxious to exceed expectations. An individual wearing a Graduate Cap isn't frightened by goals that are slightly out of their reach.

They don't say, they *do*. Your reasonable fear, having dealt with those wearing Sun Hats and Viking Helmets for so long, is that these statements might be another round of passive-aggressive deflections. After all, it's not easy to tell the difference between the Sun Hat who says "Sure, I'd be happy to." and the Graduate Cap who says "Yes, let's do it." The Viking Helmet who says, "It's coming." can be difficult to distinguish from the Graduate Cap who says, "Leave it with

me." The results that land on your desk in short order are where a Grad Student shows her true colours.

However, the Grad Student's superpowers are also their weakness. Like a Border Collie or Jack Russell Terrier, they thrive on challenge, learning and growth, but they need to be active or they're prone to destroying the couch.

A Grad Student who is not challenged will quickly seek greener pastures. A study conducted by Glassdoor, an on-line job search website, revealed that workers who stagnate in their role are significantly more likely to leave even if they are offered more money to stay. Pay will get your High Performers in the door, but it's not likely to keep them there.

Graduate Cap With a PhD

A Graduate Cap with a PhD is a high performer who thinks they know more than they really do. Ken has some close friends who work as support services professionals in university administration and who deal regularly with "PhD-itis", a disease that afflicts those who have left behind the classroom to become a department head or dean.

The most common symptom of "PhD-itis", is the assumption that expertise in a narrow field (comparative religions, for example) translates into expertise in all fields (library management systems, for instance). Sometimes this is true. Keen thinkers can bring a fresh perspective and new insights to intractable problems. Methods of addressing systemic problems in one discipline can often be re-purposed to another. "PhD-itis" arises when self-assurance passes the tipping point and blooms into over-confidence.

In short, there are dangers in winding up the Graduate Cap and letting them loose. As we'll hear, the wise leader knows the Graduate Cap with a PhD demands some adroit management as well:

1. "I thought the issue needed addressing, so I rewrote the Business Plan over lunch."

It sounds absurd, but Russell swears this is a verbatim quote from one of his clients. They reported that their team member had the best of intentions, and was crushed when their plan wasn't adopted. The risk here is that an angry retort or quick slap-down of The PhD, might result in the loss of exceptional talent.

2. "I didn't like the wheel, so I reinvented it."

A Graduate Cap with a PhD is intelligent and experienced enough to see the flaws in any system, even ones they have only passing familiarity with. They're overconfident enough to believe that there is a better, more efficient way and they're the ones who can find it. However, the Graduate Cap with a PhD, needs to learn that sometimes systems exist for a reason.

3. "I promised I'd get it to you for review, but I was falling behind so I launched it last night, so that we would remain on schedule."

Verbal marching orders and a tight timeline can conspire to give a Graduate Cap with a PhD more permission space than intended. The PhD said they'd get it done on time and at all costs and, unfortunately for you, they meant it.

4. "Instead of wasting your time with a report back, I've set up a meeting with your biggest client for tomorrow."

It's nice of them to respect your time like this but there may be consequences if you haven't had the opportunity to review their work before they present it publicly.

5. "I told your Vice-President about my idea for exceeding our targets that you kyboshed and she thought it was a great idea."

If you've never had a team member go over your head or do an end-run around you in a passive-aggressive challenge to your authority, then you may be the first in corporate history. You may also be smart enough to realize that the idea has merit and can move the company or project forward. However, it's bound to create friction between you and your star employee, if it's not handled appropriately and transparently.

This category is not solely reserved for fresh-faced millennials six months out of business school or someone who has recently returned from a training program. They could be 25 or they could be 55, so long as they've earned your trust and you've given them some autonomy. It's how they deal with that autonomy which will determine if they are a productive self-starter or a destructive Graduate Cap.

Recognizing the Graduate Cap in Your Workplace

Having read an overview of Graduate Cap behaviour, take some time now to reflect on your own workplace. Think about your own team or, if you don't have a team, consider your co-workers or a group you've worked with previously. Do you have (or have you had) an individual wearing a Graduate Cap on your team? Do you have more than one?

1. What behaviours do you see this person demonstrating that would indicate they are wearing a Graduate Cap?

_____

_____

_____

Which of the above are behaving like Grad Students? Which are behaving like they have a PhD.?

2. What phrases do you hear this person saying that would indicate they are wearing a Graduate Cap?

_____

_____

_____

3. What impact does their behaviour have on others in the workplace?

_____

_____

_____

4. On a scale of 1-10 how serious is this?

1	2	3	4	5	6	7	8	9	10
Not Serious								Very Serious	

Since employees wearing Graduate Caps are intelligent, engaged and motivated, it's easy to assume that they can also identify the behaviour that they are exhibiting and self-correct. After all, if the dynamic is so obvious to an outsider, why can't they look in a mirror, see what's happening and simply stop? It can be tempting for a leader to assume that their graduate caps will work it out amongst themselves. In fact, this reasoning assumes, they'll likely be even better off for having figured it out themselves. This is a false rationalization that even the most decorated leaders use to abdicate their responsibility. A director of several Nobel Prize-winning scientists discovered this the hard way in the 1950s, and his benign neglect resulted in a grave historical injustice. Let's see what happened when several high-functioning employees wearing Graduate Caps were left alone in a petri dish.

WHEN GRADUATE CAPS COLLIDE

Rosalind stared at the three men in disbelief. This was her research project, her laboratory time, her results, and now they wanted her work. "If you want to use my photos for your purposes," she said turning back to her desk, "you'll have to speak to Randall."

"Well, er, you see," stammered Maurice. Rosalind rolled her eyes. Maurice always stammered around her and took forever to make his point. "That's the thing. I have and ..."

*"Rosy turn around," James interrupted. "We need to F**xxx**ing talk to you! We're all on the same team."*

Rosalind slowly turned and glowered, "You're not. You're from Cambridge."

"Well, er..." James stumbled, "Randall says we should all work together."

"He hasn't told me that."

"Well," Francis jumped in, "he's told Maurice, who told us and we're telling you."

"If our roles were reversed, would you hand over all your research to a competing lab based on hearsay?"

"Uh..." now they were all stammering. What is it with these men? Rosalind wondered. All condescension and ego right up until you challenge them on the facts and then they wilt like fresh-cut lilies in the sun.

Rosalind had been excited to work with the great scientist

Sir John Randall when she arrived at his lab at Kings College London two years ago. He assigned her to supervise a PhD student but, unfortunately, he failed to tell the student's former supervisor, Maurice Wilkins, about the change. Maurice was resentful, but too passive-aggressive to bring it up. It didn't help that Rosalind had no patience for those who weren't as smart as she; and, since she was very smart indeed, this meant just about everyone she worked with, including Maurice's buddies from Cambridge, James Watson and Francis Crick.

"Maurice tells us that you've got an X-Ray diffraction photograph of such fine detail that it hints at the shape of the DNA molecules."

"It hints. That's all. And one photo isn't evidence. For Lord's sake, you're scientists. You should know that."

"There isn't time," Francis protested. "The Americans are close to a solution. We've a matter of weeks. If that."

"Francis and I are close. Our new model, has revealed ..."

"Your bunch of sticks you mean?"

She'd seen James and Francis' attempts to build a model of the structure of DNA using wooden sticks and spools, and their approach frustrated her. It was intuitive. Instinctive. Decidedly unscientific. When she had seen their first model last year, it had taken her no more than a few minutes to identify that it was backwards. The bases couldn't be on the outside because they repel water. Since water is essential for life they had to be on the inside. It's basic chemistry, and the *lads should have known it. The fact that it took a woman to point it out galled them and they didn't speak to her for almost a year. Until now, when they needed her.*

"No." Rosalind said. "You can't just play with wooden blocks and sticks and call it science. I won't let my work be party to it."

"They'll see the photos soon enough anyway," Maurice said flatly. "You've been fired. Randall's ordered you to hand over all your research materials to me."

Rosalind straightened her back. "I've not been fired. I'm moving on to a position better suited to me. One that's not riven with sexism and political infighting."

"You can put whatever feminist spin on the situation you see fit," Maurice retorted. "As soon as I get proper copies of the photographs, I'll show them to James and Francis."

"You're welcome to. Until then, they remain my photographs, my work, and I'm not sharing them with anybody outside of this lab without explicit instructions from Randall."

"By which point the American crew will have realized their mistake and cracked the structure of genetic material."

"Without any corroborating data to back it up. You're moving too fast. All of you. The important thing is the data. And that's what I'm focusing my energies on. Not all these petty politics." She turned back to her camera. "Now, if you'll excuse me, I've got to get back to some real breakthrough work."

Rosalind Franklin stuck to her guns and she never did show her work to Francis Crick and James Watson. However, on their way out of the office that day, Maurice Wilkins secretly gave the two men a sneak peek at Photo 51. It showed the interior of a cell, with DNA strands intertwining. It was all they needed. Over the next two days Francis and James fashioned a three-dimensional model to represent the now universally recognized double helix shape. They published their findings in the prestigious academic journal *Nature*, with only a vague acknowledgment that they had been, "stimulated by a general knowledge of" Rosalind's work. Maurice published a paper that appeared second in the same journal. Rosalind published Photo 51 third. The order is important because it suggested that Rosalind's work merely supported the work of the men. Ultimately, the Nobel Prize was awarded to Francis Crick, James Watson and Maurice Wilkins.

Rosalind Franklin was not awarded the Nobel because she was already dead. She was diagnosed with ovarian cancer in 1956 and despite two surgeries and radiation treatment, died two years later. X-Ray diffraction photography is finely detailed work, basically consisting of taking images of molecules. The dangers of X-ray radiation were not fully understood in the 1950s and it's assumed that Rosalind, ever the perfectionist, stood close to the X-Ray device to get the best possible images and failed to take adequate protection. As testament to her sacrifice, pioneers in the field cite her work as "amongst the most beautiful X-ray photographs of any substance ever taken".

There's much blame that goes around for Rosalind's treatment. Even though Maurice was technically allowed to show her work, the manner in which he did so was underhanded. James Watson painted a very unflattering portrait of Rosalind in his non-fiction book, *The Double Helix*, clearly still holding a grudge ten years after her death. Francis Crick was the only one of the three to mend his relationship with Rosalind, and his wife nursed her in their home after her first surgery. Even he admitted that everyone at Kings College condescended to Rosalind at every stage.

But we should reserve the greatest distain for Sir John Randall, the lab's Senior Director. Randall did not properly inform Maurice that he was re-assigning a PhD student to Rosalind. As a senior scientist and academic, Randall would have been keenly aware that PhD students were a status symbol[14]. He would have had to be blind not to see the conflict brewing between Maurice and Rosalind. Instead of addressing the problem, Randall hoped that they would eventually work it out themselves. He was an absentee boss who allowed a toxic work environment to develop in his lab where overt sexism and subtle anti-Semitism combined to leave Rosalind ostracised.

Randall's poor people management skills are now described as The Peter Principle. It states that individuals are promoted for their technical skill, not for their ability to manage teams. These are separate skills. Many companies offer technical training but don't even consider offering management training. Management training can help prevent personality clashes like the ones that plagued Randall's lab, which made

[14] Sir John Randall was no intellectual lightweight. In the 1940s he invented the cavity magnetron, which made it possible to outfit ships and airplanes with radar, a scientific feat which was directly responsible for the Allied victory in World War II. It's also the same technology that powers your microwave today.

Rosalind's work life so unhappy and tainted the discovery of the structure of DNA.

In our lexicon, Randall retired to the beach with his Sun Hat. Maurice was wearing a Viking Helmet and hiding passive aggressively behind a shield. His friend James was wearing a Viking Helmet and poking Rosalind with his sword. Francis was wearing a Sun Hat and watching it all go down from the safety of the Tiki Bar.

Though Rosalind wasn't free of blame either. She was wearing a Graduate Cap and that's not helpful headgear for collaboration. Rosalind was smarter than most of those around her, and she didn't hesitate to let them know it. She felt that her methodology was the only valid course of action, and she refused all invitations to participate with the team. Rather than sharing her knowledge when ordered to, she hoarded what she knew. She was treated abominably, but she also treated those around her poorly.

These are the dangers when employees wear their hats and remain oblivious of their impact on others.

Everyone involved in our short story was misunderstanding or misusing their power, a common complaint when dealing with employees (and bosses) wearing their Graduate Caps. Let's take a look at the different kinds of power that employees may have access to in the workplace. Being aware of the base from which we derive power and seeing how these bases overlap and interact, helps prevent this kind of conflict from festering.

WITH A GREAT POWER BASE COMES GREAT RESPONSIBILITY

Any leader's ability to influence their employees, peers and superiors is rooted in some sort of power base from which they convince, persuade or coerce[15].

Broadly speaking there are two categories of power bases which a leader can rely on for their authority: Positional Power and Personal Power[16]. Both are useful at different times, for different purposes, so it's useful to break each of these two categories down further into different sub-categories. Each overlaps considerably, and any conversation is likely to see a leader employing more than one of these bases at once.

Positional Power

As the name implies, Positional Power Bases are those tools that come with the position that a person has been hired for. There are four types of power that come with position.

Formal Power: Any role comes with a title and a corresponding position in an organizational hierarchy. The formal title carries with it a certain prescribed set of powers that a leader can exert over their particular domain[15]. A CFO usually has jurisdiction over the budget, financial planning, risk management and other financial matters. The Project Manager has jurisdiction over the individuals on their team. Any of these leaders may delegate some of their authority to

[15] Our model of Power Bases is drawn from the work conducted by social psychologists John R. P. French and Bertram Raven in 1959. Their work initially identified five bases, and later added a sixth. We've expanded the model further which resonates more fully with the experiences and needs of our clients.

[16] French and Raven called this "Legitimate Power", but that term implies that other power bases are less legitimate. A more accurate description of what they are describing is the role or formal position within the hierarchy, essentially where they sit on the "org chart".

POWER BASES

POSITIONAL POWER	PERSONAL POWER
FORMAL POWER IT'S PART OF YOUR JOB DESCRIPTION	**CONNECTION POWER** WHO YOU KNOW
REWARD POWER YOU CAN OFFER AN INCENTIVE	**CHARISMATIC POWER** WHO YOU ARE
RESOURCE POWER YOU CONTROL ACCESS	**EXPERT POWER** WHAT YOU CAN DO
COERCIVE POWER YOU CAN PUNISH	**INFORMATION POWER** WHAT YOU KNOW & CAN SHARE

others. For example, the CFO might allow the Project Manager to be responsible for the budget of a project. Essentially, if you wield Formal Power, it means that when you tell me to do something, so long as it's legal and ethical, I pretty much have to do it.

The Downside: A leader needs to be clear on the limits of their Formal Power. Issuing orders outside of one's jurisdiction can easily build resentment. If these orders are later reversed by someone with legitimate authority, it can further undermine your authority. Remember, employees are obeying the role, not the person. When the role changes or shifts, so too does the power.

The Upside: The chain of command exists for a reason. When a leader is acting within their clearly defined scope, Formal Power is efficient, decisions can be made effectively, and tactics can be executed quickly. Hierarchical command is especially useful in times of crisis. No one should be debating tactics with their superiors when they are taking fire.

Reward Power: A leader can also exert the power to reward individuals if they comply with a request. We often call this the "carrot", in reference to the stereotypical peasant farmer who convinces his reluctant donkey to move forward by holding a carrot dangling on a stick just out of reach. A "carrot" could consist of monetary rewards such as a raise or a hierarchical reward such as a promotion.

The Downside: A leader often can't control salary increases or promotions by themselves and there is a risk in making a promise that you may not be able to fulfill. Furthermore, studies show that financial reward only motivates individuals to a certain point; once basic financial needs have been met, other rewards are necessary.

The Upside: There are other kinds of non-monetary rewards that a leader has at her disposal which can be deployed with some imagination. These include the ability to work from home, time off in lieu, inclusion on a more interesting research project, or a cubical with a window.

Resource Power: A leader who has access to needed resources can offer a similar kind of "carrot". These might be desirable assignments, training opportunities, funding approval for a pet project, a new computer, or any number of other material resources that an individual has a need for.

The Downside: A leader overusing resource power to force compliance could be viewed as petty. Russell recalls a manager whom he worked for early in his career in the UK who was responsible for office supplies. She kept the key to the supply cupboard closely guarded and insisted on seeing your spent pen before she'd let you have a new one. If access to resources is an effective motivating tool in your organization, then it implies that you have employees who are keen on their work. If this is the case, it raises a dilemma; if you have access to resources that improve an employee's ability to get their work done more effectively and enthusiastically, *why on earth would you as a leader, withhold them in the first place*?

The Upside: If a leader approaches the exercise of Resource Power as a negotiation, then they can agree that certain unsavoury tasks must be completed because they have priority. Once those tasks are completed or in progress, then the requested resources can be freed up for the more interesting work.

Coercive Power: This is the "stick" that our peasant farmer might use to motivate his donkey when the "carrot" fails. Threats and punishments such as demotions, firing, or disciplinary action are common coercive tactics that leaders may use.

The Downside: With an overuse of these tactics, a leader could be accused of bullying. It may result in an unpleasant workplace, which only serves to encourage your best employees to leave.

The Upside: Coercion doesn't have to verge on bullying. Calmly outlining the consequences of a certain course of action could, in and of itself, persuade someone to change their actions. A leader might even make a persuasive and logical argument that would encourage someone to step into line.

Leaders must recognize the limitations and dangers of all varieties of Positional Power as it's only half the story. Exercising only Positional Power bases inevitably results in a cold, technocratic organization. Remember that you're dealing with humans after all, not Vulcans. A great leader knows they must also leverage their Personal Power.

Personal Power

In contrast to the Positional Power that is connected to an organization's hierarchy, Personal Power is all about the individual. It's simplistic though to think that personal power is purely about being likable or charismatic. We all know great leaders who aren't warm and fuzzy, but whose teams would follow them into the fire. These qualities, which often seem amorphous and indefinable, can be quantified. Once they're understood, they can be leveraged just as deliberately as the elements of positional power.

Connection Power: These Individuals accumulate power through their associations with others[17]. They may derive their power from personal connections to other leaders, affiliations through their political parties, or because they represent a constituency or group. These are also the mavens or connectors in your sphere who seem to know everyone. Looking for a referral to a consultant with an obscure expertise? They've got a name. Want tickets to the playoffs? A person with Connection Power can not only get you tickets, they'll ensure the team mascot stops by your seats for a selfie.

[17] French and Raven called this "Referent Power", because an individual's power exists in reference to their connection to others. Again, language usage has changed over time, and we feel the term "Connection Power" is clearer.

The Downside: An individual with Connection Power is at the mercy of those connections, and when they vanish it has an immediate negative impact on their power base. The sheen can also wear off over time. Notice how quickly individuals disavow their connections to someone who is tainted by scandal.

The Upside: Humans are social creatures and are driven by a powerful need to belong. Your Connection Power accumulates the wider your web of connections spreads, becoming a self-fulfilling prophesy.

Charismatic Power: This is power that individuals accumulate because people like them, want to be like them or just want to be near them. We all know people who draw others into their orbit through sheer force of their natural personality.

The Downside: Charisma can be used to exclude people. Many of us have experienced the clique in high school, led by a charismatic individual who uses a threat of social exclusion as a coercion tactic. It's vile when it happens intentionally in a supposedly mature workplace, but even those with the best of intentions can inadvertently exclude others. Every in-group also has its dark side, the out-group.

The Upside: A leader who wields Charismatic Power intentionally and strives for inclusion, can make everyone feel good in their presence. This tends to draw out the best in everyone.

Expert Power: Individuals who possess specific, unique and rare expertise are often looked to as leaders. These are the subject matter experts that everyone has in their organization, such as the senior employee who has weathered a similar storm or the young hotshot who knows the ins and outs of the new software.

The Downside: Expert power must be earned and maintained. It requires focus and attention to stay up-to-date on the current trends and best practices. It also requires the Expert to maintain credibility, which can lead them to making bold assurances when a more cautious and nuanced approach might be required. I'm sure we've all encountered the pompous expert who uses their Expert Power to bolster their ego and put down others. Even when ego isn't involved, Expert Power can threaten others' self-esteem. Under-confident leaders can sometimes view Expert Power as a threat to Positional Power bases.

The Upside: A wise leader acknowledges expert power and makes it work for them. The modern military is particularly flexible at applying Expert Power. At the heart, any military is a profoundly hierarchical organization, but in the field, even leaders defer to experts when the situation demands it. A Lieutenant or Sergeant may outline the objective of the mission (i.e. clear the field of landmines) but they defer to those with expertise when it comes to the execution (i.e. everyone follows the demolition expert's instructions.)

Informational Power: Individuals who possess information, have a power base that is somewhat similar to those who hold Expert Power. However, in the case of Information Power, the base is external to the person and so the power can be shared or given away.

The Downside: Since information is not intrinsic to the person, this power base is precarious; it lasts only so long as the information is current. If the precious information becomes out-dated or is proven to be inaccurate, then the power is quickly eroded. The Information Power base also relies on its relative scarcity, which can prompt an individual to hoard information and use it as a tool for reward/coercion.

The Upside: The old saying "information is power" is equally true in the workplace. Since most decisions depend on accurate, reliable and trustworthy information, those who hold information have an incredibly influential base of power. A wise leader knows that this base is most potent when it is widely shared throughout the organization.

Let's take a moment with the following worksheet to examine which of these power bases are at work in your work life.

Recognizing Power Bases at Work in Your Workplace

Having read an overview of Power Bases, take some time now to reflect on your own workplace. Think about your own team or, if you don't have a team, consider your co-workers or a group you've worked with previously.

1. Which Power Bases do you feel you operate from in your workplace? Place an estimated percentage to indicate how much of this power you have access to:

___% Formal Power–its part of your job description.

___% Reward Power–you can offer an incentive.

___% Resource Power–you control access.

___% Coercive Power–you can punish.

___% Connection Power–who you know.

___% Charismatic Power–who you are.

___% Expert Power–what you can do.

___% Information Power–what you know and can share.

2. Knowing that you have access to power is different form exercising it. Circle which of the above power bases you have access to but use most rarely.

3. Why do you think you use it less often?

_____

_____

_____

4. Identify three individuals in your workplace, either on your team or elsewhere, and identify the power base they most consistently operate from.

i. _____   _____

ii. _____   _____

iii._____   _____

Getting Power Right

Ken worked closely with a dynamic and magnetic leader who we'll call Betty. Betty had recently been promoted to a new role as Vice President and Chief Operating Officer and began making an impact almost immediately. Her dynamic personality made her engaging and her ideas for change energized those around her. The staff enthusiastically engaged with the many new projects she launched.

She made a point of wandering the building every Friday afternoon, an activity she dubbed "doing the rounds". She would chat casually with staff, inquire about what projects they were up to, and offer helpful suggestions if required. She was tireless in her support of the many teams to which she had assigned new projects.

After a period of some months, Ken noticed that one of the teams he was consulting with, had pressed pause on the development of a project in order to collect feedback from stakeholders via a survey after a suggestion from Betty. This team had already held several focus groups and convened several town hall meetings, through which they had gathered a good deal of input. They had even begun synthesizing the results. When Ken asked why Betty was insisting on a survey, no one was able to provide an answer. So, Ken took it upon himself at his next one-on-one to challenge Betty on the effectiveness of a survey at this stage. "Oh, I'm not married to it one way or the other," Betty replied. "I was just floating the idea."

Betty had felt she was simply suggesting the idea in the spirit of brainstorming. However, she failed to account for the increased formal power base that came with her new job title in this new workplace culture. Betty had come from a director role in a very large organization where she had limited formal power. As a leader she fostered a collaborative approach amongst her team and relied on her charisma to motivate and galvanize the managers who reported to her. Now, as VP and Chief Operating Officer, Betty's "suggestion" was taken as a command and "doing the rounds", was viewed as checking up on those commands.

Shocked at the havoc she had wreaked with an off-handed comment, Betty and Ken began to re-examine her assumptions about power bases. Ultimately Betty decided she didn't want to change her working style, but she needed to be intentional about cultivating a new workplace culture. She continued to brainstorm with her teams and doing the rounds on Friday afternoons, but she made sure that the staff understood that she wasn't issuing instructions or monitoring their work, but simply trying to get to know everyone and provide support.

Betty came to understand that a leader has multiple power bases that they can use at any given time. A change in power bases is common with a new role, and a strong leader learns to recognize and be intentional about how they use that power.

Relying too heavily on any one of these eight power bases is not a good strategy. If a leader loses access to resources that they have previously used to persuade others, then they may be abruptly powerless. If a leader relying on charismatic power finds themselves confronted with someone who doesn't like them for whatever reason, they may find themselves unable to be effective. However, when any two or more power bases are combined, leaders are more likely to be resilient. When Positional Power bases are combined with Personal Power bases, leaders can weather multiple shifts in the economy, in the workplace or in their lives. They can be influential, resilient and a pleasure to be around.

It's also vital that we understand that leaders are nothing without followers. Even if a leader does not actually have the power they're exercising, if their followers *believe* they do, a leader is effectively wielding power. For instance, a leader may not actually possess technical expertise in a specific area, but the team needs to feel their leader has sufficient background to make an informed decision. A leader usually doesn't have the absolute authority to fire someone on a whim, but the majority of employees recognize that their superiors possess the ability to take disciplinary action that would lead to their dismissal. So, an unspoken social contract evolves in which we confer a power base on others. Recognizing the existence of a social contract illustrates the precarious nature of these power bases. A wise leader cultivates multiple power bases and deploys them sparingly in ways that are appropriate to each situation.

Let's take a look at a fictional scenario, as we have with each of the other hats in our paradigm. In Act Four, Scene One we will meet Andrea, the new CEO of Riverside General Hospital and Luis the CEO of the Riverside Hospital Foundation. Andrea has inherited a structure she doesn't like, in which the Donor Relations Department has been sep-

arated from the hospital itself, to create an autonomous foundation. Luis, a young leader brought in by the former hospital CEO, has developed the organization's structure, written its terms of reference and recruited its inaugural board.

As you read through the scene and the subsequent analysis, try to infer what power bases you see at work.

ACT FOUR, SCENE ONE

Lights up. Luis enters, trying hard to supress a bounce in his step. Andrea frowns. Luis' smile fades.

ANDREA: I just heard about Richard Morales.

LUIS: Oh. I'd hoped to tell you myself.

ANDREA: Morales is very happy to announce that he's donating $5 million to the Riverside Hospital Foundation for the Spinal Injury Trauma Research Chair.

LUIS: For starters. I'm convinced there's more money on the table down the road.

ANDREA: He's so happy he's already announced it. On Facebook.

LUIS: Oh, that's premature. I'll send him a text and ask him to delete the post.

ANDREA: And his people have already sent a draft press release to our Publicity Department.

LUIS: The fact that he has "people" who can generate a press release overnight suggests that there might be more money on the table.

ANDREA: You mean, for our Spinal Injury Trauma Research Chair?

LUIS: Don't worry. We'll make sure that it's also for "associated administratrivia".

ANDREA: We don't have a Spinal Injury Trauma Research Chair.

LUIS: We will soon.

ANDREA: At Riverside General we don't do spinal trauma research.

LUIS: It's an important cause.

ANDREA: It's not one of our strategic priorities.

LUIS: Then we should make it one.

ANDREA: I thought you were going to ask him for $50,000 for the new wing?

LUIS: I asked him to add a zero. In the end, I got him to add two.

ANDREA: We talked about this. You can't just ask a donor to "add a zero". You'll scare him off.

LUIS: Except I didn't. Look, you haven't been to the Morales home. You walk in their living room and he's got a Rothko on his wall. A Rothko. Most of those paintings are in museums or corporate offices, and there aren't that many in private hands. And on the wall opposite, he's got two photos of Robert Mapplethorpe by Patti Smith. Autographed. To him. Personally. This house is dripping with money and he's not scared to spend it in ways that lets everyone know he has it. Of course he can add a zero.

ANDREA: You almost crossed a line. You're lucky he didn't pull his donation altogether.

LUIS: There comes a moment in every conversation with a donor where you just know that it's time to up the ante. Otherwise, we're never going to reach the big goal.

ANDREA: There's a process to follow.

LUIS: And sometimes the process takes a back seat to instinct. Donations are about human relationships and human relationships don't follow a process - there isn't a science to fundraising, as much as we wish there was. It's people giving to people.

ANDREA: We don't need a Spinal Injury Trauma Research Chair. We don't want a Spinal Injury Trauma

Research Chair. Why isn't the money going into the new wing?

LUIS: Because Spinal Injury is a subject he's passionate about.

ANDREA: Get him passionate about another subject. A subject in line with our strategic priorities.

LUIS: It's not that easy.

ANDREA: You're a persuasive guy. You got him to add a zero.

LUIS: I got him to add two zeros for spinal research because he's in a fxxxing wheelchair.

ANDREA: There's no need for that kind of language.

LUIS: I think there is. You're telling me to turn down a -

ANDREA: I'm not telling you to turn down anything. I'm telling you to redirect the -

LUIS: Which is going to kill the deal. So, you are effectively telling me to turn down the fourth largest donation this Hospital has received.

ANDREA: Don't exaggerate.

LUIS: I'm not. Five million dollars is the

single biggest gift since we created the Foundation. In fact, it's the fourth largest donation in the entire history of the hospital. I know because I checked before I went into the meeting.

Pause.

ANDREA: So, it was premeditated? Asking him to add two zeros?

LUIS: Well... I thought about it a little bit beforehand. I did some research. I'm not a maverick.

ANDREA: So, you went against my direct instructions?

LUIS: What do you mean "instructions"?

ANDREA: I told you to ask him for a reasonable donation because I knew that otherwise we'd end up promising more than we can deliver.

LUIS: I think you mean you suggested the ask. Because, after all, you're not my boss.

ANDREA: I'm the hospital's CEO.

LUIS: You do remember that the foundation is a stand-alone entity, with its own board?

ANDREA: A board of which I am a member.

LUIS: As an ex-officio appointment. Not as Board Chair. I talked to my Chair about the fact that there might be a possibility to ask for a larger donation. And she agreed.

ANDREA: So, you did an end run around me?

LUIS: How? By strategizing with my own Board Chair?

ANDREA: This is the kind of thing my child would have done when she was six. If she didn't like the answer I gave her, she'd go ask Daddy and try to get a better answer.

LUIS: Did you just compare me to a six-year-old?

ANDREA: Only because you're acting like one. When it comes to both fundraising and board relations, we have to be on the same page, to ensure we are in alignment with our strategic plan.

LUIS: The goal of our strategic plan is to raise enough money to build a new wing for the hospital.

ANDREA: Without jeopardizing basic operations in the process.

LUIS: How does a cash infusion of five million dollars jeopardize the operations of an entire hospital?

ANDREA: Because you've just made a ton of more work for us-

LUIS: It's all handled by the Foundation. And, yes, I'm sorry about the press release. We'll take care of it. We'll even handle processing of the cheque. I'll minimize the impact on you.

ANDREA: It's not so simple as saying, "We'll create a new research chair." Creating a chair and then funding its research properly - not to mention finding the right candidate - is a massive project. In the end it could cost millions.

LUIS: Now who's exaggerating?

ANDREA: I've been working in hospital administration all my life. I know what I'm talking about.

LUIS: It's a gigantic hospital. It's a behemoth. It's not like we don't have resources.

ANDREA: With all the recent cuts, we operate pretty close to the bone.

LUIS: Not that close, surely.

ANDREA: Fundraising in a small city is a

delicate ecosystem. And when you're a lumbering beast with a skeleton staff in a fragile forest, anything can have a major impact on the environment. Scandal can kill you. An erosion of trust can starve you. Success can bloat you beyond your capacity.

LUIS: You're afraid of success?

ANDREA: I don't mean that exactly. Just… we have to be cautious. We've got a seven-year window to fundraise for that new wing. Let's use the entire runway. Slow growth is manageable growth.

LUIS: Slow growth is boring. I don't want to be in an organization that isn't rapidly growing.

ANDREA: Then maybe your time is up.

LUIS: Again, I point out to you that you're not the boss of me. I had a strategy, I talked to my board chair about it, I acted on my gut and it paid off. My boss is my board chair. Do you think my chair is going to turn down a $5 million donation? We'll see whose time is up.

Luis stands calmly and exits the office. Andrea wakes her computer and angrily starts typing an email.

Evaluation

Now that you've had the opportunity to watch a Graduate Cap in action, let's analyze what we've observed and how it differs from the other hats.

1. In your opinion was Luis:

☐ The Graduate Cap Grad Student?　☐ The Graduate Cap with a PhD?

List three behaviours you observed which convinced you of your choice.

_____

_____

_____

2. Which power bases did Andrea operate from? Place an estimated percentage, indicating how much of each she used.

☐ Formal Power ___%　　☐ Connection Power ___%

☐ Reward Power ___%　　☐ Charismatic Power ___%

☐ Resource Power ___%　　☐ Expert Power ___%

☐ Coercive Power ___%　　☐ Information Power ___%

3. Identify three things that Andrea could do to help Luis be more effective.

_____

_____

_____

4. If you had the opportunity to coach Andrea on how to approach Luis about his behaviour, what is the single most important piece of advice you'd give?

_____

_____

_____

That Went South Fast

Andrea's conversation with Luis started on a sour note and went downhill from there. Let's analyze what wasn't working for Andrea before we offer advice on what steps she could have taken to make it a more productive conversation.

The biggest issue is that Andrea isn't being forthright with Luis, on multiple levels. She is angry from the moment he walks in the door, but she doesn't come out and say it. It's a full page before she even mentions the issue of the research chair. By withholding information and her feelings, she is manipulating the conversation, using her knowledge to situate herself as an authority, and attempting to exert her power over him. This is bound to leave Luis feeling increasingly entrapped and condescended to, as the conversation unfolds. In fact, power is what lies at the heart of this conflict.

This is one situation in which it might actually have been less damaging to start with, "I need to f**xxx**ing talk to you!" While it might not have been tactful, at least it would have surfaced the issue immediately.

You may feel that because Luis has not been forthright himself, Andrea is justified in feeling angry about the situation. Or you may feel that she is being needlessly territorial. Both points of view are valid. How you feel about Andrea's decision can offer insight into your leadership style. Whichever position you take, we hope it's clear that Andrea's emotional response is not helpful to the conversation, and serves only to escalate the situation.

Don't get us wrong; it would be unhealthy for Andrea to

bottle up her feelings. Multiple studies have shown that suppressing anger can have a detrimental effect on one's health. Apart from the cost to your personal health, there's also a cost to organizational health. Not being forthright about how strongly you're feeling about issues can leave employees wearing a Graduate Cap prone to minimizing the seriousness of a situation in their zeal to push ahead. This leaves them open to being blindsided later when you fully vent your pent-up frustration. Remember that Andrea is the leader. It's her responsibility to articulate her feelings, in a controlled manner, to ensure that everyone knows where they stand.

The best way to do that with a Graduate Cap is to acknowledge that there are two sides to every story. Doing so means that you, as the leader, have to go first. It's up to you to make an effort to see the other side, as well as your own. In the process of articulating both sides, you're much more likely to win them over to your point of view. And in the process, you might actually convince yourself there are merits to what your employee is trying to accomplish. Regardless of hierarchy, Graduate Caps are emerging leaders, and should be treated as such. You're likely to get more from them if you adopt a co-creation attitude rather than authoritative one. Remember that two brains are better than one. After all, you're the boss; why should you be the only one doing all the heavy lifting?

Consider how Andrea approaches the situation with Luis. She has not acknowledged his victory, nor even made an effort to do so. He's clearly very proud of what he's accomplished, and he's got a right to be pleased. He turned a $50K donation into $5M through insight, strategy and sheer force of personality. By not acknowledging what he has accomplished, she prompts him to exchange his Graduate Cap for a Viking Helmet.

Luis and Andrea definitely have two different worldviews. Andrea views slow growth as manageable growth and wants to use "the entire runway". Luis says, "I don't want to be in an organization that isn't rapidly growing." That's ok. However, Andrea needs to acknowledge that there are differences between their views and use those differences as a springboard to understand. She clearly doesn't know her colleague very well and it's almost as if she's not spent any time to get to know him.

Andrea is using Formal Power, behaving as if she is Luis' boss, when it's pretty clear, that she has no authority to do so. She attempts to use Coercive Power when she drops a veiled threat ("maybe your time is up") but it backfires. Blinded by her conviction that she was justified in using her Positional Power, Andrea ignored all the Personal Power bases (Connection, Charismatic, Expert or Information), which could have helped her.

Many leaders become so accustomed to the ease of communication that comes with command-and-control hierarchies, that they attempt to apply it to all situations. Just like the proverbial round peg in a square hole, it doesn't always fit.

Evaluating Your Own Graduate Cap

Have you always been coachable? Being coachable means being open to feedback.

1. Has there ever been an occasion when you have not been open to feedback or took feedback personally?

_____

_____

_____

2. Were you wearing your Graduate Cap with a masters degree or a PhD? What behaviours did you demonstrate?

_____

_____

_____

3. If you had the opportunity to go back in time and coach your old boss on how to call you out on your behaviour, what is the one piece of advice you'd give her/him?

_____

_____

_____

4. Was there a time when you were VERY coachable? What did you or others do that made you open to receiving feedback?

_____

_____

_____

INFLUENCING IN ALL DIRECTIONS

A few years before Russell moved to Western Canada he was working in London England for "Scotland Yard"[18]. Russell was part of the Leadership Development Team, charged with building the capability of senior leaders within the police. Particular attention needed to be paid to the manner in which they communicated and exercised influence with the world outside of the police force.

At the time that Russell was contracted by the Metropolitan Police, it was reeling from the Stephen Lawrence Inquiry and the impending MacPherson Report. Stephen Lawrence was a Black British teen from Plumstead, south-east London, who was murdered in a racially motivated attack, while waiting for a bus on the evening of April 22, 1993. The police investigation was later found to have been marred by professional incompetence, institutional racism and a failure of leadership. Even before the report was released, it was widely recognized that the force had not kept up with the pace of change. One of the key recommendations of the report was the need for senior police leadership to partner with communities and other external agencies and their traditional communication style wasn't going to cut it.

Police officers are often trained, like military personnel, to give and receive orders. Following the inquiry, the leadership of the police force needed to address the manner in which they communicated internally with their peers, civilian support staff, and with other divisions within the force. As well, they had to communicate externally with other law enforcement agencies such as HM Customs & Excise, Home

[18] Technically, Russell was working for the Leadership Development Team of the Metropolitan Police, which was based out of a structure a couple of blocks away from the actual building referred to as New Scotland Yard. Though Ken insists on telling everyone that "Russell worked at Scotland Yard" because it's way cooler.

Office and police services of other municipalities and communities.

The Director of Leadership Development Programs and Russell's boss was Fergus Lawson, a sharp dresser with a big personality and a sharp mind, not always a welcome combination in the days when the Force tended to be suspicious of those not in uniform. Nevertheless, after months of careful relationship building, Fergus succeeded where others had failed by creating a simple model that could be quickly understood and implemented to achieve immediate results.

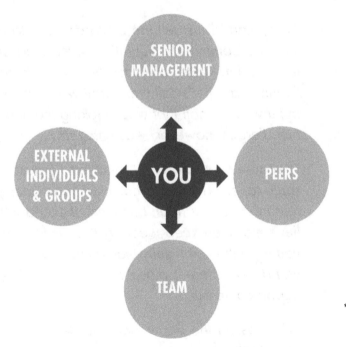

The model*, above, illustrated the Four Directions of Influence that any leader has to understand to communicate effectively. Essentially, he took their usual linear direction of

*Graphic created by Fergus Lawson and used with permission.

communication and bisected it with a horizontal axis. On one end were placed internal communications (Peer Borough Commanders, other law enforcement agencies, etc.) and on the other, external communications with the community (community leaders, city hall, MP's, etc.).

Together Russell and Fergus began to explain what is now obvious; you need to apply a different method of communication for each of the four directions. Let's eavesdrop on one of the typical conversations that Russell and Fergus held with the Borough Commanders:

"Why can't I just tell the bastards what to do?" said the Commander squinting at the diagram in front of him. Russell could tell the veteran Borough Commander (let's call him Brian) was half-joking, but it was the half that wasn't joking that worried him. Fergus, however, was unfazed.

"Because, you old sod," retorted Fergus in the same tone. "The world has changed under your feet in case you hadn't noticed. If you don't believe me, then keep wearing that uniform when you meet the community leaders in Newham. The world's a different place since the MacPherson Report came out."

Brian tossed the paper onto the desk in front of him, took off his cap as he sat down and regarded Fergus critically.

"Okay you cheeky bugger, tell me what I've got to say."

Fergus tapped the diagram on the desk. "This is you in the centre, right? You can push commands down this way, that's easy. Look it's nearly lunchtime, so let's suppose the order is about a sandwich. You tell your officer 'Get me a sandwich'. It's a command. The only acceptable response is 'Yes'. But how do you influence up?"

"May I have a sandwich, Sir?" Brian laughed, "I'm not sure I influence up at all."

"That's crap, Brian. You do it all the time. When you want to get the Deputy Commissioner to back off on a dopey idea, what do you do?"

"Well, I... I give him a better option. Or a few."

"Right. Maybe it's a salad. Or soup. But if he says it's a sandwich, then it's a sandwich, right? So, there's a number of possible choices he can make, but the choice is his alone, right? So, let's go this way, to the right side. Suppose you need a sandwich from the Home Office. Is it a command?"

"No."

"So, what is it?"

"It's a request."

"'Would you please make me a sandwich is a request. It's called Social Contracting[19]. It's what makes life happen."

[19] This application of the term "Social Contracting" is borrowed from The Primes by Chris McGoff, John Wiley & Sons, 2012. www.theprimes.com

"That sounds like a big HR word for telling some-one what to do."

"That's your problem right there Brian. You're using a command with the community leaders in Newham, when you should be making a request. REQUESTS invite responses of either 'no' or 'yes'. Both responses must be acceptable."

Brian rocked back in his chair and interlaced his hands behind his head. You could almost watch the penny drop.

Fergus continued, *"Social contracting is made up of three elements that are often undistinguished from each other. The first element is the 'Statement'. 'There is a protest' is a statement and re-quires no response. 'Get your riot shield', is a command. The only acceptable response is 'Yes'."*

Brian picked up the thread, *"But 'Would you please organize a meeting so I can speak with the youth group', is a request. And if it's a re-quest, then I have to be prepared that 'no' is a valid response, even if I am police."*

"The problem is, too often these elements are not distinguished. People use STATEMENTS when they are really making REQUESTS or even COMMANDS. Healthy organizations distinguish these three elements and require leaders to use

each element appropriately, depending which way they're working this diagram."

Given the dialogue above, it might seem that Fergus was audacious, to start this change initiative with the Borough Commanders. "I picked the parts of the organization where I had the best chance of a win," Fergus revealed in a recent retrospective interview. "The Borough Commanders had a resource team of their own under their command which included not just uniformed officers, but civilian employees working in Finance, HR, and admin. In addition, the Borough Commanders interacted with a lot of groups internally and externally and it was increasingly clear to them that what they were doing wasn't working. So, they had a burning need for change. Basically, they had opportunity and motive." Still, it took a lot of work initially to persuade key Borough Commanders that this was the approach to take and not all were in favour. Once they were converted, Fergus and Russell could use the Borough Commanders as the champions to fight the battle elsewhere in the organization.

With Fergus' persistence, Russell watched the Borough Commander population learn to value this model. The Boroughs they were working with started performing better and delivering better than others. Fergus leveraged this success to show that it was the appropriate leadership model for many roles. This attracted the attention necessary of others and slowly other parts of the business came on board of their own volition.

How would history have been different if Maurice Wilkins had set aside his sexism and enmity and recognized

Rosalind Franklin as a peer with whom he needed to adopt a different communication style, in the spirit of the Four Directions of Influence? Or if Sir John Randall, the Laboratory Director, had not abdicated his leadership responsibilities and had recognized that different power bases were at play within his workplace? Of course, we'll never know. We can however find out how the scenario between Luis and Andrea could have unfolded differently, if Andrea had been aware of these models.

Recognizing Four Directions of Influence in Your Workplace

Thinking of your own organization, try to identify individuals internally whom you receive commands from and those you give commands to. Continuing to think internally, who are peers whom you cannot simply give commands to and must instead make requests of? Finally, who is external to the organization whom you cannot simply give commands to and must instead make requests of?

Who INSIDE of the organization do you receive COMMANDS from?

_____

_____

_____

Who OUTSIDE of the organization do you make REQUESTS of?

_____

_____

_____

SENIOR MANAGEMENT

EXTERNAL INDIVIDUALS & GROUPS — YOU → PEERS

TEAM

Who INSIDE of the organization do you make REQUESTS of?

_____

_____

_____

Who INSIDE of the organization do you give COMMANDS to?

_____

_____

_____

ACT FOUR, SCENE TWO

Lights up. Luis enters.

ANDREA: I just heard about Richard Morales.

LUIS: Rats. I'd hoped to be the one to tell you myself.

ANDREA: Luis, I have to tell you I'm upset.

LUIS: Excuse me? You're upset about a $5 million windfall?

ANDREA: I know you're excited and I'm sorry to be the one to rain on your parade, but this raises some serious issues.

LUIS: This is a major contribution.

ANDREA: You think I don't know that?

Andrea catches herself and takes a breath.

Just a moment. I need to collect my thoughts.

Silence. Luis fumes, but Andrea takes the time she needs to compose herself.

Let's start again. I know you've worked hard at developing the relationship with Richard Morales, which has made this donation possible. That's an incredible achievement.

LUIS: But…?

ANDREA: But… this gift is not in alignment with our strategic goals.

LUIS: So, let's make it a strategic goal.

ANDREA: I think you know it's not that easy. But let's set the practicalities aside for one moment, because this situation is indicative of a larger issue, and if we can address that, we may be able to circle back to a solution.

LUIS: What's the larger issue, then?

ANDREA: The Foundation is not in alignment, with the Strategic Goals that have been set out in our five-year strategic plan.

LUIS: I don't see how you can say that when the Foundation - me, I - have just secured the fourth largest donation in the history of the entire hospital.

ANDREA: Again, I'm not denying that it's a significant achievement. I'm suggesting that it may not be the right achievement. More importantly, I'm saying that the actions of the Foundation are not in alignment with our goals.

LUIS: You mean my actions are not in alignment with our goals.

ANDREA: I do actually. Yes. Your actions with regards to this donation are not in alignment with our goals.

LUIS: It's five million dollars.

ANDREA: I don't care if it's 5 trillion dollars or five thousand dollars, the issue is still the same. Actually, I do care, it's a lot of money, that's why I'm here to discuss our strategic priorities, so that we can work it out. Look, let me give you an example of what I mean about alignment.

LUIS: Please.

ANDREA: Three things. To begin with, we don't need a Spinal Injury Trauma Research Chair, we don't want a Spinal Injury Trauma Research Chair and we can't afford to create one from scratch, no matter how big the gift. What we desperately need is the new hospital wing that we are already publicly committed to building.

LUIS: OK, so -

ANDREA: I'm sorry to cut you off Luis, but it's important that you see the big picture before we dive into each example. Can you agree to hold that thought?

LUIS: Uh… Sure.

ANDREA: Secondly, you went in to ask him for $50,000 but turned around and asked him for $5 million.

LUIS: I asked him to add a zero. Two zeros.

ANDREA: That's a lot of zeros for something that, as far as you know, the rest of us may not be able to deliver on. Do you see how by not acting in alignment with strategy, and failing to communicate with us, you've potentially put our joint reputation at risk?

LUIS: No, I don't.

ANDREA: What happens to your reputation if Morales discovers that you've taken a cheque for something that you can't deliver on?

LUIS: Obviously, the gift is pledged over five years.

ANDREA: So how do you think it's going to go over when you need to tell him that you asked him to increase his donation by a factor of one hundred for something that doesn't exist and can't be created within five years?

LUIS: Huh.

ANDREA: The third way in which we're not in alignment is between you and I more directly. We sat right here in this office last week and we made a plan together about how to approach Morales for $50K and what it would be targeted towards. Subsequent to that, you had a conversation with the Board Chair -

LUIS: There is nothing wrong with talking to my Chair about the fact that there might be a possibility to ask for a larger donation.

ANDREA: Except that, because of the complicated relationship between the Foundation and the Hospital, she sits on my Board as well. So, when you make a plan between you and her, that is at loggerheads with what you and I have previously discussed, you're effectively hanging me out to dry.

LUIS: I don't see how I'm hanging you out to dry.

ANDREA: When my Board Chair calls to tell

me that Morales announced this donation for the Spinal Injury Trauma Research Chair, I have no clue what to say because I'm expecting a donation for $50K for the new wing. And I'm the one that has to explain to him that we don't even have a Spinal Injury Trauma Research Chair. I have to explain to the Board Chair why Morales' people have already sent a draft press release to our Publicity Department.

LUIS: OK, that sucks.

ANDREA: It does, indeed, suck. It sucks eggs. So, let's reiterate the effect that not speaking with "one voice" has. There's the capacity to fulfill the promise you've made to the donor. There's the reputational risk to both the Hospital and the Foundation. There's the reputational risk we both face by not speaking with one voice to our boards. And finally, because the donation is really needed for a building fund, we are now behind where we should be.

LUIS: And how much of this is about Andrea being pissed off that I'm stepping on her toes?

ANDREA: You know, to be honest, some. I'd like to think I owned up to those feelings when we began this conversation, but if I wasn't clear then let me say it now. I'm angry that we're not in alignment and I'm scared at the potential consequences. More to the point, I'm hurt because we're not working together. We could be doing so much more if we were moving in step with one another.

LUIS: Well, thank you for owning that, at least.

ANDREA: Luis I'd like you to understand that you don't operate in a vacuum. This isn't about me stamping my authority on the Foundation. Nor is it about quashing your victory. It's about appreciating the political considerations of working in a complex organization. Every decision you make has an impact on others, both within and outside your sphere of control.

LUIS: Yeah. Sure.

Luis slumps dejectedly in his chair.

ANDREA: This has been a difficult conversation, hasn't it?

LUIS: Kind of… I mean… I came in on cloud nine prepared to celebrate and it certainly hasn't turned out that way.

ANDREA: No, it hasn't. And I'm sorry about that, even if it doesn't seem that way to you right now.

Silence.

Maybe we've come far enough for one day. What do you think?

LUIS: Maybe.

ANDREA: Why don't we let this sink in and reconvene tomorrow?

Luis stands and starts towards the door.

LUIS: That's maybe a good idea.

ANDREA: Two things we have to deal with before you go.

Luis pauses with his hand on the doorknob.

Number one, Morales' premature Facebook announcement.

LUIS: I'll ask him to delete the post.

ANDREA: Thank you.

LUIS: What's the second thing?

ANDREA: May I leave you with a question?

What outcome would be ideal? Don't answer now. Feel free to sleep on it.

LUIS: All right. I'll think on it.

ANDREA: OK. And Luis?

LUIS: Yeah?

ANDREA: Let's use this incident to move forward together.

LUIS: That'd be good.

Evaluation

Now that you've had the opportunity to watch Andrea take a second shot at her conversation with Luis, let's analyze what we've observed.

1. Which Power Bases did Andrea operate from this time? Place an estimated percentage, indicating how much of each she used.

☐ Formal Power ___%

☐ Reward Power ___%

☐ Resource Power ___%

☐ Coercive Power ___%

☐ Charismatic Power ___%

☐ Expert Power ___%

☐ Information Power ___%

2. Did Andrea have a:

- Challenging Conversation (proceed to question 3)
- Coaching Conversation (skip to question 4 below)

3. If you thought Andrea was having a Challenging Conversation, then re-read Scene Two, looking just at Andrea's lines. Try to identify at which points she is:

- speaking about Luis' BEHAVIOUR
- providing EXAMPLES of his behaviour.
- identifying the EFFECTS of his behaviour.
- requesting different behaviour in the FUTURE.

4. If you thought Andrea was having a Coaching Conversation, re-read Scene Two looking just at Andrea's lines. Try to mark out the points when she is:

- describing the CURRENT situation.

- defining the OUTCOME.

- identifying what ACTIONS are possible.

- asking CRITICAL questions about those actions to prepare Luis to make an informed choice.

- asking Luis HOW he plans to be accountable for success.

5. By the end of the dialogue how likely do you think Luis is to change?

1	2	3	4	5	6	7	8	9	10
Not Likely								Very Likely	

Peeking Behind the Curtain

In Scene Two, Andrea took the time she needed to compose herself. Starting off on the right foot made a huge difference, just as it had for Raj, Kendra and Dan before her. Andrea was even more committed to regulating her emotions than her predecessors. She paused the conversation when her temper was getting out of control. Luis fumed, which could have backfired, but it was more important that Andrea remain in control of the conversation.

Andrea acknowledged Luis' success early in the conversation, something she failed to do altogether in Scene One. Later in the conversation she also acknowledged she was feeling angry and scared. These are not easy feelings to own up to in a workplace. Being vulnerable showed Luis why she was upset and allowed him to empathize with her to the point where he admitted that the situation in which he'd placed her "sucked". This was an admission that Luis never would have made in Scene One.

Andrea also took the time to clearly identify the central issue for herself, just as Kendra had in Act Three, so that she could avoid laying out a list of grievances. In this case, Andrea identified that the issue was that they were not in alignment. It's worth noting that Andrea's initial way of wording the misalignment was not entirely genuine. She attempted to soften the conflict by stating that, "The Foundation is not in alignment with the Strategic Goals that have been set out in our five-year strategic plan." Luis challenged her wording of this statement by boldly stating, "You mean *my* actions are not in alignment with our goals." To her credit, Andrea admitted that he was right. Andrea's admission gave Luis a small win, and it didn't undermine her argument or cost her much in the way of social capital.

Andrea also stated her goal was to get to a point where they could work more closely together. You'll recall that we recommend you use language that bolsters the working relationship rather than creates discord. Andrea does this when she states, "I'm here to discuss our strategic priorities so that we can work it out." And, recognizing that Luis is dispirited and might forget this key point later, she reiterated it again at the end of the conversation by stating, "Let's use this incident to move forward together."

In the evaluation worksheet at the end of Scene Two, we asked if Andrea was having a CHALLENGING or COACHING conversation. We feel she is having both. She was challenging Luis and used the B.E.E.F. Model throughout much of the conversation.

- She began by outlining the *behaviour*: "Your actions with regards to this donation are not in alignment with our goals."

- She continued by providing three *examples*; Luis committed them to creating something they can't follow through on; he increased the size of the ask from $50K to $5M; he acted unilaterally.

- She clearly stated the *effects* to the organization, to her and to Luis himself.

- She suggested some short-term *future* actions he could take which included reconvening the next

day and in the meantime, dealing with the Facebook post.

Andrea's last question, what outcome would be ideal, was the beginning of a COACHING conversation. She wisely suggested they take a break, but she planted a seed that could germinate in their next conversation. This is known as the Hemingway Effect, named after the famous and prolific writer. Ernest Hemmingway would leave a sentence unfinished, with the paper still in the typewriter, so that he could kickstart his next day's writing by completing a thought. Andrea left Luis with the same task; an unfinished thought that they could begin with during the next conversation.

Let's see what happens when they reconvene.

ACT FOUR, SCENE THREE

*Andrea takes one last look at the boardroom
table. She has set out a small meal: quiche,
vegetables, salad, sparkling juice and some
pastries for dessert. It's not much but spread
out on the boardroom table, it looks surpris-
ingly inviting. When she turns around, Luis is
already at the door. Andrea steps back in surprise. Luis looks at the table set with food.*

LUIS: Oh. I thought we were meeting in
here?

ANDREA: We are. I stopped at the bakery this
morning and… well, I got carried
away.

LUIS: That's very nice of you. Thanks.

ANDREA: There's no point in hammering this
out on an empty stomach.

LUIS: I suppose…

Andrea invites Luis to sit.

ANDREA: So; let's break it down. We've got a
situation. We were pretty clear
yesterday with what's going on.
We've thought about it overnight.
Tell me, what impact is the current
situation having?

LUIS: We're in conflict. Barely speaking
to one another.

Luis puts down his fork and pushes his plate away.

> And I can't finish this gorgeous quiche.

ANDREA: Yes, OK, well, beyond that?

LUIS: As you've made abundantly clear, I've secured us a donation that's not meeting our needs. And it might cost the hospital more money to execute on than the value of the actual donation. AND you think we're not aligned strategically.

ANDREA: You said that "I think." Does that mean you disagree?

LUIS: I just... I still don't see these two goals as incompatible.

ANDREA: All right. Then let's make that one of our objectives for this conversation: to see if we can align the Morales gift with the strategic priorities. In the process, maybe we can get our two organizations more closely aligned in their goals. Can we agree on that?

LUIS: Yes. I can get behind that.

Luis seems to relax a little at this. He reaches for his fork.

ANDREA: What obstacles are holding us back from achieving that tomorrow?

LUIS: Morales wants to fund a research chair and we want a new wing.

ANDREA: Is he really stuck on a research chair?

LUIS: No... I think he wants to fund research. He told me that because his personal experience with the health care system in the region was so bad, he doesn't want anyone else to suffer through that.

ANDREA: OK, so that's actually a different situation. He wants to secure a better life for those with spinal injuries and he sees research as the way to do that.

LUIS: Yes... that's an accurate summary of his thinking.

ANDREA: So, what obstacles are holding us back?

LUIS: The fact that he's fixated on "research". There might be other avenues I haven't explored which can help him achieve his goal. And, yes, before you say it, I see where you're going with this. These other avenues might be more aligned with the strategic plan.

ANDREA: So, let's start with the most blue sky idea we can. If anything was possible, what would you do?

LUIS: Raise enough for this new wing through 10 major gifts rather than 1,000 small ones.

ANDREA: That's *very* specific.

LUIS: Well, I've put some thought into it. It's my job after all.

Luis leans forward.

I'm not saying we ignore small gifts, but strategically, there's more to be gained from going after the big fish because it creates buzz and drives the smaller donations. Take care of the big fish and the small fry follow. I still believe that there are the resources in this community for the 10 major gifts. Look at the increase in the tech sector that we've seen in the east district.

ANDREA: Do you remember when we finished our meeting yesterday, I asked what outcome would be ideal? I imagine you've put some thought into that?

LUIS: I have. We get Morales to pivot from funding a spinal injury research chair to funding better care for

those with spinal injuries. Then we use Morales' gift to give the campaign for the new wing a kick in the pants.

ANDREA: Funny, now that I've calmed down a bit, I was thinking the same thing. A Rehab Unit is in our strategic plan. Not until phase 3 of the new wing, but still, it's in there. What steps have you already taken towards your goal?

Luis reaches for his plate and spears a piece of asparagus.

LUIS: I haven't…

ANDREA: Come on, I know you. You've not only made up your mind, you're moving ahead with something…

LUIS: OK, I've been cultivating relationships with three different tech firms here in Riverside. The industry historically does not engage in any significant philanthropy.

ANDREA: They don't? I keep hearing about the Bill Gates Foundation…

LUIS: It's actually the Bill and Melinda Gates Foundation. She does most of the work. Actually ,it's a classic example of how philanthropy works in the tech industry.

Luis brings his plate a little closer. Andrea sits back a little.

> The companies don't put very much emphasis on community investment or corporate social responsibility, but the individual tech founders, the Presidents and Vice Presidents, do. They build a company, they cash out and then they're sitting on a big pot of money. It's not until that point that they're happy to spread it around. But here's the thing; it's not about the company making strategic investments in the sector in a targeted way. It's their personal money, and they spend it on their pet projects.

ANDREA: Like Morales.

LUIS: Like Morales. And that's why the personal touch is so important.

ANDREA: And so, what you need to do next is…?

LUIS: Use Morales as my point of leverage. Use his passion to sway others in the community. He's very admired across the entire industry because he founded TechGiant.com.

ANDREA: What would you do if time were not an issue?

LUIS: THIS is exciting. Recently several firms in California have founded the Silicon Valley Foundation. This Foundation funds activities around the world, not just in the Valley, so we are technically eligible. It's going to take time, but Morales has nothing but time now that he's sold TechGiant.

ANDREA: Is this an option you feel ready to act on?

LUIS: Absolutely.

ANDREA: What's the best way you've handled something like this in the past.

LUIS: It's the kind of thing I did a lot of at Lincoln Centre. Use one respected donor who has a passion project and turn him or her into your ambassador. If you get them wound up, then you can just sit back and let them do the work. You have to guide them, but you can let them do the heavy lifting.

Luis puts down his fork and pushes his empty plate away.

ANDREA: What do you think you need to do next?

LUIS: Take our new donor to a meeting at the Silicon Valley Foundation. If I can get Morales to help us get a donation from them, then I can use both Morales AND this foundation to pressure our local tech companies into donating to our wing. Not as individuals, but as companies.

ANDREA: This is very exciting. Now here comes the toughest question. You and I came into conflict because of the Morales donation. Fantastic though it was, it was not aligned with the strategic plan. What have you decided to do differently as you move forward?

LUIS: We prove to Morales that it's a spinal rehab centre, instead of a research chair, that is going to get him what he really wants. Better quality of life for all concerned.

ANDREA: That's Morales, but what are you and I going to do differently as we move forward?

LUIS: I think we're going to have to communicate better. To make sure that any new philanthropists who come on board don't push us off course, like Morales did. At the same time, we need to invite them to take ownership of the project, and some times that means inviting their input. It's a tricky balance.

ANDREA: What do you need from me?

LUIS: Some trust. Trust that I know what I'm doing. That we can make these seemingly outrageous conditions that come with these gifts work for us.

ANDREA: I can see that. Perhaps more clearly then I ever have before, as a result of this conversation. I'm very impressed with your plan. Really, I am. There's something I need though, so I can be comfortable offering the trust you're requesting; I need to be kept in the loop.

LUIS: That's fair.

ANDREA: If I'm informed before the fact, not after, and if I'm assured that we are both aligned in our work, then I can trust. Even better, I can support. So, with that in mind, what three things will you do differently?

LUIS: Three? How about if we just agree to keep one another up to date.

ANDREA: Yes, sure. But how?

LUIS: Let's… what if we have lunch regularly? Like this.

ANDREA: That would be nice. Every two
           weeks?

LUIS: How about once a month?

ANDREA: Can we start with every two weeks
           until we get the Morales thing
           sorted out, and then scale back?

LUIS: Sure.

Luis reaches for the dessert tray.

ANDREA: If everything goes well how will
           our working relationship be
           different?

LUIS: We'll have our new wing inside of
           five years, and we'll be working
           together to do it, instead of at
           cross purposes.

ANDREA: I'd like that.

LUIS: Me too. Do you want to split these
           desserts? I can't decide between
           them...

Evaluation

Now that you've had the opportunity to watch the C.O.A.C.H. Model in action, as Andrea coaches someone who is not a direct report, let's analyze what we've observed.

1. On a scale of 1–10, how successful do you feel Andrea was in using the C.O.A.C.H. Model with Luis?

1	2	3	4	5	6	7	8	9	10

Not Successful   Very Successful

2. Re-read Act Four, Scene Three, just looking at Andrea's lines. Try to mark out the points when she is:

- describing the CURRENT situation.
- defining the OUTCOME.
- identifying what ACTIONS are possible.
- asking CRITICAL questions about those actions to prepare Mario to make an informed choice.
- asking Luis HOW he plans to be accountable for success.

3. Why did Andrea choose to ask the questions she did?

_____

_____

_____

Now let's take a moment to consider Luis:

1. How likely do you think Luis is to remain on course strategically?

1   2   3   4   5   6   7   8   9   10

Not Likely   Very Likely

2. What support do you think Luis now needs from Andrea to remain accountable?

_____

_____

_____

Reviewing the Buffet

It's no mistake that Andrea brought lunch, even if it was an impulse buy. Meeting over food is always a positive idea, because something special happens when we break bread together. Studies show that those who eat socially more often are more trusting of others and are more engaged. When people are eating the same food, they are more likely to trust one another[20]. It's doubtful Andrea knew the science when she bought an extra quiche at the bakery that morning. However, like many of us, she knew instinctually that sharing a meal with Luis would be a good idea.

When they got down to business, Andrea didn't start with the question she'd left him with ("what outcome would be ideal".) Instead she followed the first step in the C.O.A.C.H. Model, making sure to outline the current situation first, to assure they were both on the same page.

In proceeding through the model, Andrea let Luis be the expert even when he was being condescending. Andrea was wise to keep her cool and let him flesh out a plan on how to proceed. This is a strategy that works well with a Graduate Cap because, unlike a Hard Hat, these individuals are experts in their own right. Andrea's strategy was to ignore his passive aggressive need to prove his intelligence, and use his knowledge to arrive at a solution.

In Scene Two, Andrea had identified a lack of alignment as the core issue which lead to Luis' maverick behaviour. She stuck with that topic in Scene Three and persisted in prompting Luis until he recalled that particular issue. Throughout the

[20] A study published in Adaptive Human Behaviour and Physiology, shows that groups of employees who eat together have higher levels of trust (R.I.M. Dunbar, *Breaking Bread: the Functions of Social Eating* , September 2017, Volume 3, Issue 3, pp 198–211). Work at the University of Chicago goes even further and suggests that *what* we eat matters. In one of their experiments, they assigned volunteers the role of either a manager or a union representative. When the volunteers ate the same kinds of food, the parties reached agreement much more quickly. In another part of the study, the researchers had volunteers listen to someone offering a product testimonial. When the participants were eating the same food, they were more likely to trust the information in the testimonial (NPR, Morning Edition, February 2, 2017. Also, supporting evidence from Alice G. Walton, *Chicago Booth Study Examines How Family-Style Dining Boosts Cooperation* UChicago News, Dec 18, 2018).

conversation, she continued to return to the goals of the strategic plan in subtle ways to keep him on track. This was important because, for all his brash talk about strategizing to secure donations, Luis displayed a tendency to get tactical rather than strategic. He wanted to solve the Morales problem and get moving. There was a solution at hand, and Andrea could have simply leapt to the solution and moved on, but her more methodical approach may reap long-term benefits. To riff on the old saying: you can give a person a fish and feed them for a day, or you can teach the same person to fish and they'll stay out of your hair for a lifetime. In the same way, a leader who only provides their Graduate Caps with tactical solutions, finds themselves returning to the same problems with eerie repetition. Leaders who lead their Graduate Caps with strategy, start to build autonomy, independence and resilience.

A LEADER CAN COACH ANYONE

It may come as a surprise to hear that you can coach someone who is a peer in, or is part of, an external organization. After all, even people who are not part of your company can wear a Viking Helmet, Sun Hat, Hard Hat or Graduate Cap. If you see them approaching wearing such headgear, you would be foolhardy not to take evasive action. Be cautious: it would be very easy to offend someone's ego by overstepping your boundaries. However, this is what the C.O.A.C.H Model is useful for. You're only asking questions, after all. Coaching through asking questions isn't giving commands. It's not even making requests. It's a conversation aimed at finding common ground. The model is called the Four Directions of *Influence* for a reason. One has to be wary of overtly guiding the conversation towards a predetermined outcome. Your intentions are key. You need to approach the coaching conversation with a genuine interest in where it will go.

SUMMARY

Individuals wearing a Graduate Cap can be grouped into two broad categories:

- The Grad Student who has learned from work and life and has the confidence to take initiative.

- The PhD who has mastered their field, who has too much confidence and thinks they know everything.

Any leader's ability to influence their employees, peers and superiors is rooted in some sort of power base from which they convince, persuade or coerce. Broadly speaking, there are two categories of power bases which a leader can rely on for their authority; Positional Power and Personal Power.

Positional Power Bases:

- Formal Power
- Reward Power
- Resource Power
- Coercive Power

Personal Power Bases:

- Connection Power
- Charismatic Power
- Expert Power
- Information Power

Relying on any one of these bases is precarious. When any two or more power bases are combined, leaders are more likely to be resilient. Followers are essential. The authority that a leader exerts, either relies on or is strengthened by, the belief of the followers.

Communicating within a hierarchical structure is generally clear, as it follows a command and control model. The same methods cannot be used when communicating with peers within the organization or with individuals who are external to the organization. The Four Directions of Influence is a useful communication model for each of the four directions.

It's possible to use the C.O.A.C.H. Model with someone who isn't a direct report, but it requires skill to navigate hazardous waters.

EPILOGUE

Everyone Hates A Rehearsal

Like so many people in business, Russell and Ken hate rehearsal, practice, dry run, role-play, or whatever other phrase you choose to call this activity. It seems to be the second most dreaded activity in corporate training, right after "audience participation". Our antipathy is all the more shocking because in our Managing the Unmanageable workshops, we use both scenarios *and* audience participation. We do it, even though we hate it when it's done to us, because studies have shown that it works.

Learning something and applying what you've learned in a relatively safe environment, engages different areas of the brain and accesses multiple learning styles. This active involvement results in processing of information at a deeper level than mere memorization can achieve. A rehearsal or role-play results in "episodic memory"; a deeper kind of memory specific to an event. The result is that someone like Mario, doesn't have to remember an idea or technique; he can reconstruct it from the powerful memory of the event that he has physically and emotionally experienced.

In Act Three, Scene One, Mario confessed that he has trouble with the B.E.E.F. Model when in the heat of the moment. It's not so much that he has trouble *remembering* it (it is, after all, four words connected by a memorable mnemonic), but that *he gets lost when it comes time to execute it*. When dealing with Jerry, he struggled to control his temper, lost track of what he was saying and, as a result, fell back on old habits. A dry run of the conversation would reinforce the skills, and give him an opportunity to plan how he wants to address the issue.

However, many people don't role-play well. When thrown into a situation, they can be nervous and not particularly enthusiastic. They tend to approach it half-heartedly in the hope that it will be over as soon as possible. Or, like Mario, they are afraid to do it wrong and over-compensate by being robotic. This is why, when we offer these workshops, we almost always hire a trained actor to play the individual wearing one of the four hats. Our actor is instructed not to relent until the participant convinces them. They're skilled in improv, so they respond to any curve ball the participant tries to throw at them. Our scenarios are detailed enough that if the participants solve one issue, they're armed with a storehouse of further complications to keep the scenario moving.

It's also helpful to have a third person acting as mediator. When we run these workshops for our clients, Ken or Russell can call time out and invite the participant to reflect on how the conversation is going, seek help from the audience, and even rewind the scene just like in the fictional scenarios in this book. The role of this third person is vital in keeping the role-play on track.

We do recognize that we're not entirely superhuman and we can't be everywhere at once.

So, with that in mind...

A FEW GUIDELINES FOR SUCCESSFUL ROLE PLAY

It's always possible to role-play with your colleagues, but it's always uncomfortable for the first few minutes, even if you're used to it. So just accept that it's going to be embarrassing for the first ten minutes. We have found that the following tips help start off on the right foot.

Identify the Situation: Be clear on the problem that you're trying to work through, and make sure that both you and your coachee know what you want to achieve by the end of the session. In plenty of cases, such as in the situation Dan faces with Mario, this will be based on a real-life problem that the coach and coachee are facing together. Reviewing this before beginning, will help people to start thinking about the problem before the role-play begins.

Add Details: Next, set up a scenario in enough detail for it to feel "real." In particular, make sure that everyone is clear on the location. This allows the coachee to begin to settle into the "reality" of the role- play. It also stresses to the coachee, the importance of ensuring the right environment when it comes time for the actual conversation to take place. For instance, Mario didn't plan a location in his mind ahead of time, so when the situation arose in a public setting, he simply pursued the conversation without thinking through the consequences of where all this was taking place.

Assign Roles: Once you've set the scene, identify the various characters involved in the scenario. Some of these may be people who have to deal with the situation when it actually happens (for example, Mario has to speak to a foreman). Others will represent people who are supportive or hostile, depending on the scenario (for example, Jerry is defensive and gets angry). Often there are no more than two or three characters required. In fact, it's usually best with only two.

Use an Audience: Recruit someone who can also act as an audience member. Something different happens when we role-play in front of a neutral third party. If you've ever had the good fortune to be present in the rehearsal hall of a theatre, you can see this in action. Actors can be running lines and working on a scene with one another. They may run quickly through some parts, at half speed through others and stop and start on a whim. But as soon as the director enters, the focus shifts in a way that is immediately palpable. Everything is suddenly more serious; the stakes are higher and breaks less likely. Inviting someone to sit in on your rehearsal is giving yourself the gift of focus.

Let it Build: It can be useful if the scenario builds in intensity. For instance, if the aim of your role-play is to practice a challenging conversation, the person playing the role of the unmanageable employee, could become increasingly defensive and difficult. This allows you to test and practice different approaches for handling situations. In our Forum Theatre for Business workshops, our professional actors are trained to give our participants a "win" when they first replace a fellow participant, but then to present the participants with a second challenge. Beware of making the first "win" too easy. If your coachee always succeeds, no matter how unrealistic their role-play, then no one is really benefiting. We learn from confronting and overcoming a challenge. Our actors are trained to only give a "win" when they feel their character has genuinely been convinced to change their point of view.

Go First: It's useful if you, the coach, start the role-play. That way you can keep the scenario on track to meet your learning objectives. In our workshops we always invite our professional actor to give the first line. Otherwise we find our participants devolve into small talk to set themselves at ease. In real life, it is necessary to build an empathetic bond with your unmanageable employee, but it's less important in a fictional role-play. Really, we think it's just an unconscious way of procrastinating.

Say "Yes And": Remember the exercise explored earlier during the Intermission. You're not helping your partner if many of the offers they make are met with "No". This is called "blocking" and, just like in gridiron football, it doesn't help you move down the field.

When you finish the role-play, discuss what you've learned, so that both you and your coachee can learn from the experience. Having said that, you can also pepper some learning throughout the role-play. There's nothing preventing you from calling a time-out to discuss what's happening. After discussing, you can provide some coaching and ask questions that let your coachee find their own answers. Then it's time to rewind the scenario and take another run at it. These "stop/starts" (as we call them in the theatre) afford opportunities for real-time learning and allow your coachee to implement what they're learning directly.

Remember to be just as clear when you re-start, as you were the first time. It can be tempting for a coach to leap right in to keep the momentum going. However, don't forget the coachee is simultaneously recalling what they said during the first take, absorbing new instructions in preparation for the second take, and trying to use their imagination to transport themselves into the circumstances where the scenario is set. That's a lot of mental activity going on at once. You can help them out by being extra-clear with your instructions. Phrases such as, "let's back up to when I said such and such" or "let's take another try at explaining the example of his behaviour on Wednesday", are very specific and clear. Avoid vague instructions such as, "let's start from when you got confused" or "go back to the bit about the examples".

You may know exactly which example, or which turn of phrase you're thinking of, but your coachee might be thinking of something else entirely.

No matter what role you're playing, remember to have fun with it. We all learn better when we're having fun. As they say in the theatre, it's called a *play* for a reason.

ACKNOWLEDGEMENTS

Thanks first and foremost to all of the participants who have bravely marched to the front of the room to take the hot seat in front of their peers. It's never easy to demonstrate a new technique while you're still integrating it, and we recognize you for trusting us with your learning journey.

Thanks to all of our pre-readers who took time out of their busy schedules to read an early manuscript version of this book and provided invaluable feedback. Among them: Dean Jetten, Marnie Kirkwood, Fergus Lawson, Jane Joseph and Paul McIntyre Royston. Your input was invaluable. Our editor Cheralyn Doell and designer Peter Moller, for their professionalism and guidance.

A special acknowledgement of all the actors we've worked with over the years: Peter Strand Rumpel, Nicole Zylstra, Andrew Phung, Renee Amber, Karen Johnson Diamond, Jason Lewis, Ken Gardener, Michael Roik, Michael Dargie, Jeff Gladstone, Ali Foggart, Jana O'Connor, Chantal Perron, Kevin Kruchywich, Gary Kirkham, Jesse Gervais, and anyone else whom we've worked with but neglected to mention by name. Each of you have contributed to the growth and development of our understanding of how to communicate the delicate art of navigating difficult workplace conversations.

And finally we must thank those closest to us. Ken's wife Rita, who has always believed in him; Russell's wife Alison who braved the high seas to move their small family to Canada; and his two daughters Ellie and Hannah who've become excellent hockey players.

RESOURCES

Many of the resources mentioned in this book can be found on a website that we have co-created called: **www.ineedtof-ingtalktoyou.com**.

Here we post resources that support our many programs. From this site you can:

- order B.E.E.F. cards.
- order C.O.A.C.H. cards.
- book a workshop.
- listen to our poscast
- enrol in our online course
- request a 1:1 consultation with Ken or Russell.

As well, you can read the many blogs, articles and resources that connect to the themes in this book.

In addition, we both stubbornly maintain our own corporate identities and our own websites. We work together on our Forum Theatre for Business suite of programs, the Future is Coming workshop, The SHIFT Method and a number of other initiatives. We also maintain healthy boundaries and just as often work independently. You can find out more about Ken on his website **www.corporate-culture-shift.com**. You can find out more about Russell on his website **www.bluegemlearning.com**.

ABOUT THE AUTHORS

Ken Cameron and **Russell Stratton** have together created the Forum Theatre for Business series to help organizations give their employees the tools they need to co-create a respectful workplace culture and empower individuals to challenge disrespectful behaviour. Courses include: Managing the Unmanageable, Coaching for Results, Leading From the Middle and Respect in the Workplace.

Ken Cameron

One of Ken's clients gave him the title, "Facilitator of Thinking Differently", and he's proudly hung onto it ever since. Other official titles have included, "Artist in Corporate Residence" and "Citizen Raconteur." All of which tells a story about Ken's unique contributions to creating dialogues that matter, strategic planning that surprises, and workplaces that don't suck.

Ken comes to his creative approach as a consultant facilitator honestly. In addition to a Master of Fine Arts degree Ken is one of Canada's most successful playwrights, directors and arts administrators. Since 2012, Ken has used his creative background to design sessions that draw out all participants, especially the most introverted, who rarely have the opportunity to share their thoughts. He uses his administrative experience and endless curiosity, to fully understand the business so he can reframe your focus and increase your profitability. The unique combination leads to interactive and engaging sessions that result in key insights and eureka moments.

Ken is a certified LEGO® SERIOUS PLAY® facilitator and is the co-creator of several facilitation workshops including the Future is Coming, the SHIFT facilitation card deck and the cultureSHIFT Method. His work has been recognized with a Facilitation Impact Award (Platinum Award) by the International Association of Facilitators and Organization of the Year Award by the International Association of Public Participation (Canada) for The Cultural Transformation Project/City of Calgary.

Russell Stratton

As a "Leadership Champion", Russell provides leaders with a practical toolkit for building engagement and improving individual and team performance, that will ultimately drive up the business results in your organization.

Using live actors in a stop/start forum theatre for business approach and a combination of dynamic experiential learning techniques in his workshops, participants come away with a greater ability to actually perform better as employees and leaders in their organization.

Russell has achieved international success as a result of his proven track record over the past 30 years. He has extensive experience in HR and Operations Management, in a wide range of organizational cultures, including small, medium and large enterprises. This covers a variety of industries such as construction, engineering, manufacturing, hospitality, law enforcement, local and national governments, and non-profits.

Russell is an Internationally Certified Trainer, Leadership Coach and Conference Speaker with a Masters Degree in Human Resource Management. He has a passion for developing leaders including those transitioning into management roles, by building their capability and confidence using a blend of simulations, dynamic experiential learning and workplace coaching. He is a Master Facilitator for Bluegem Learning's ground breaking 'Leadership Success' workshop series. *I Need To Fxxxing Talk To You - The Art of Navigating Difficult Workplace Conversations* is his first book.

CPSIA information can be obtained
at www.ICGtesting.com
Printed in the USA
BVHW052047231220
596313BV00001B/5